Discover
the
Adirondacks
2

Discover
the
Adirondacks
2

Walks, Waterways
and Winter Treks in
the Southern
Adirondacks

Barbara McMartin

Photographs by the Author

New Hampshire Publishing Company
Somersworth

An Invitation to the Reader

With time, the old roads, paths, and trails mentioned in this guide may be rerouted or become overgrown, flooded by beaver activity, or otherwise obscured. Trailheads and signs may be moved and landmarks altered, either by man or nature. If you find that changes have occurred along the routes described in this guide, please let the author and publisher know so that corrections can be made in future editions. Other comments and suggestions are also welcome. Address all correspondence:

Editor, *Adirondack Series*
New Hampshire Publishing Company
Box 70
Somersworth, New Hampshire 03878

International Standard Book Number: 0-89725-012-5
Library of Congress Catalog Card Number: 79-90812
©1980 by Barbara McMartin
All rights reserved

Discover the Adirondacks, 2 is a completely revised edition of *Walks and Waterways,* originally published in 1974 by the Adirondack Mountain Club. In addition to incorporating changes that have occurred over time, this edition is substantially rewritten and includes new material.

Printed in the United States of America
Published by New Hampshire Publishing Company
Somersworth, New Hampshire
Back cover photograph by Alec Reid
Design by Wladislaw Finne

Photograph on page 2: Sherman Mountain Cliffs

Acknowledgments

In the years between the original publication of *Walks and Waterways* and this completely revised edition, many people have written to say they enjoyed the guidebook and a few have told me of new places to explore. I appreciate all their comments.

My family and many friends have helped recheck the walks and canoe trips or research the winter potential of the routes. I know they did it because they love adventures in this area as much as I do, but their help was invaluable.

I want to say a special thank you for help with the revised guide to John Baringer, Shirley Cocker, Kay Hampshire, Lawrence and Maryde King, James Lenney, Willard L. Reed, Sr., Alec Reid, Ray DeRossi, and Howard and Anna Ulman.

Contents

Introduction

The third largest block of the Forest Preserve in the Adirondack Park is certainly the least known and contains some of the wildest lands in New York State. It lacks the high peaks of the Marcy area and the long interconnected waterways of the Fulton Chain. There are surprisingly few marked trails, but there are as many quiet lakes and streams and fields of wildflowers as in any part of the Adirondacks, and there are far fewer people. Spring and fall bring fishermen and hunters who rarely venture far from roads, and campers use a few of the more accessible lakes, but here hikers can explore endlessly, rarely meeting another person.

This solitary paradise is a little better known than it was in 1974 when I wrote the first guidebook describing the area, but it still holds some of the least used areas of the Adirondacks. With the exception of a half dozen trails that have become popular, the routes I walked again to prepare this revised edition are as beautiful, quiet, and free of other hikers as they were earlier. Using this guide, amateur explorers can still find hidden paths, new routes, and a variety of secret places.

It seems incongruous that an area only 20 miles from the Mohawk Valley and so near large centers of population can remain so little known. Historical development of the Adirondacks explains in part the area's slow growth as a center of recreation.

Because the region lies so near the Mohawk Valley, its forests were easily harvested for lumber and tanbark. When the forests were depleted in the decades around the turn of this century, huge blocks of land were acquired by the state, leaving little for private development.

The railroad north from Utica to Old Forge and on to Blue Mountain Lake and Raquette Lake opened the forests to the west and north to eager vacationers in the second half of the nine-teenth century. Lakes George and Champlain and later the traditional overland routes in their valleys opened the eastern Adirondacks and provided access to the spectacular High Peaks. While these routes brought people to the northern and eastern Adirondacks, the southern areas covered by this guidebook — the northern half of Fulton County and the southern half of Hamilton County — still have few roads.

The principal access to this area, Route 10, also bisects it. The road, also called the Canajoharie-Caroga Lake Road, follows an old Indian trail and the course laid out in the early nineteenth century by surveyors accompanied by Nick Stoner, a famous trapper. Until a few years ago this route into the wilderness remained poorly paved and little used. As a result, all but a few dedicated sportsmen avoided these woods. Many of the interior paths are less well traveled now than when the area was logged.

A road from yesterday roughly delineates the western boundary of the area covered by this guide. Following the valley of the East Canada Creek, the Powley-Piseco Road stretches from the town of Stratford north to Route 10 near Piseco, and much of it is still rough and unpaved. Route 30, which runs roughly parallel to and just east of the West Branch of the Sacandaga River, is the eastern boundary.

In the first edition of this guide, I included a few isolated spots north of Piseco Lake. Because this book is part of a series that will eventually cover all of the Adirondacks except the High Peaks Region, the boundaries of the area covered in this revised edition have been straightened to conform to the encircling roads. All the places mentioned are now south of Route 8, which borders Piseco Lake. Several new paths and routes in the Wild Forest area near the southern edge of the Adirondack Park have been added. The Park's southern boundary, the so-called Blue Line that now appears on most maps of New York State, is also the southern boundary of the area covered in the revised edition.

In this six-hundred-square-mile area, there are nearly a hundred small uninhabited lakes and ponds. With less than a 1,500-foot change in elevation, it holds few spectacular mountains; nevertheless, there are several exciting peaks. The revised guide details bushwhacks to some of them, routes that are described for the first time.

There are many shallow ponds and lakes, and, consequently, many typical quaking bogs. Because most paths follow rivers or streams through valleys to lakes and ponds, they are relatively

12

flat and, to their detriment, often wet. However, they provide easy routes to many good adventures. Best of all, two of these rivers meander through broad flood plains so that their valleys can be easily explored on leisurely canoe trips.

Land surrounding the East Canada Creek and the West Branch of the Sacandaga River is so little known that this guide will not only introduce you to the terrain but to the history of the region as well. Stories about the first settlers are interwoven with descriptions of locations of mill sites, tanneries, and abandoned roads.

The broad valleys and the connections between the myriad ponds also entice winter sportsmen. A majority of this guide's level trails can serve as wilderness ski-touring routes. And the few mountains in this area with cliff-top views require only gentle climbs and are sometimes best enjoyed in winter on snowshoes.

If you love the woods you will find here details of many kinds of natural delights, lakes and streams and waterfalls, wildflowers and bogs, and rocky ledges and picnic spots. Instead of dramatic climbs, you will find paths leading to quiet places to explore or sites of rare beauty along the waterways. A few paths wind into deep woods with no destinations at all. These are good nature walks, strolls from which to enjoy beauty in microcosm.

How to Use This Guide

Years ago, logging roads crisscrossed much of this wilderness, leading to numerous settlements in what is now the deep woods of the Forest Preserve. Dams were built for mills or for log runs at the outlets of many small ponds and lakes. Most of the trees cut were softwoods for lumber, pulp, or tanbark, and few hardwoods were removed. But the flurry of logging in the middle of the nineteenth century ended when the stands of hemlock and pine were felled. With the advent of chemicals for the tanning industry, most logging ceased and the woods began to reclaim the roads and houses.

A majority of the routes described in this guide were once these *logging roads.* In the south, some have been recut and reopened as snowmobile trails; hence they are marked and easy to follow. Others have been traditional routes for sportsmen, so hikers can follow the footpaths along them. However, many that are still depicted on the United States Geological Survey (USGS) topographical sheets or on other sportsmen's maps are invisible to all but the most skilled woodsmen, and after attempting to explore

13

some I almost believe they exist only in some map maker's imagination.

In this guide, a route is considered a *trail* if it is so designated and maintained by the state. This means it is routinely cleared and adequately *marked* by official New York State Department of Environmental Conservation (DEC) trail markers.

Paths are informal and *unmarked* routes with clearly defined foot treads that are easy to follow. However, paths are not necessarily kept open, and fallen trees sometimes obliterate their course. Those that cross wet meadows and open fields often become concealed by lush growth. You should always have a map and compass when you are following an unmarked path, and you should keep track of your location.

If you do find that a footpath has become so obscured you are having difficulty following it, there is a formula for proceeding. In a group of three or more hikers, stringing out along a narrow path will permit the leader to scout until the path disappears, at which point at least one member of the party should still be standing on an obvious part of the path. If that hiker remains standing while those in front range out to find the path, the whole group can continue safely after a matter of moments.

The paths did not only develop along logging roads. Sportsmen have their favorite routes to lakes and streams, and these little publicized paths are the source of many of the walks in the guide. Because of their origin and the fact that there have been few attempts to mark trails for hikers, the paths all follow fairly flat routes and are very different from the trails of the High Peaks Region.

The DEC has recently introduced a new type of route, the *marked footpath.* The concept is experimental, and two test marked footpaths have been laid out within the area covered by this guide. The inspiration for a marked footpath derives from the method in which traditional sportsmen's paths evolved. If a destination was truly desirable, a fishing hole or a distant pond for instance, sportsmen soon wore a path to it. They often used blazes to mark the way. The marked footpaths are at present flagged with plastic tape.

A marked footpath is a marked route and nothing more. It is expected that sufficient use will soon create a path. No attempt has been made to clear the route or keep it open. If the destination is really desirable, the path to it will be kept clear by those who use it.

Old *blazed* lines or trails are occasionally described. The word

14

blaze comes from the French *blesser,* meaning to cut or wound. Early loggers and settlers made deep slashes in good-sized trees with an ax to mark property lines and trails. You will often see these vertical cuts in trees and should learn to recognize them.

Later, hunters and fishermen often made slashes with knives, and although they are not as deep as ax cuts, they can still be seen. Following a blazed route is challenging; most often only portions are visible. I have walked with sharp-eyed hunters who have followed blazed paths for miles in dense woods where I could only spot a handful of the blazes. Please remember that it is now and has been for many years illegal to deface trees in the Forest Preserve in this manner.

Occasionally you will see a line that is marked with splashes of yellow paint on trees at eye level. Such lines normally indicate the boundary of private and public lands. Individuals have also used different colors of paint to mark informal routes. Although it is not legal to mark trails on state land, this guide does refer to some such informally marked paths.

Trails leading to Kane and Cathead mountains are the only two official routes whose destinations are high places with distant views. Most of the panoramic vistas can be reached only by *bushwhacks,* so some of these routes are described in order to give variety to walks in the area. Only simple details are given for the bushwhacks, because they require a degree of technical knowledge. Suggested routes for bushwhacks are shown on the maps, however.

To *bushwhack* means to make your way through the woods without trail, path, or visible foot tread of other hikers and without markings, signs, or blazes. Bushwhacking usually involves following a route chosen on a contour map using a compass and stream beds, valleys, abandoned roads, or obvious ridges as guides. Most bushwhacks in this guide require both navigating by contour map and compass and by understanding the terrain.

A bushwhack is defined as *easy* if the route is along a stream, the shore of a lake, a reasonably obvious abandoned roadway, or a similarly well-defined feature. A short route to the summit of a hill or small mountain can often be easy.

A bushwhack is termed *moderate* if a simple route can be defined on a contour map and followed with the aid of a compass. Previous experience is necessary. Compass directions are given in *degrees from magnetic north* (degrees magnetic) unless otherwise stated.

A bushwhack is rated *difficult* if it entails a complex route, requiring advanced knowledge of navigation by compass and reading contour maps and land features.

Distances along all the routes are measured from the USGS topographical sheets and are accurate to within 10 percent. Few hikers gauge distance accurately even on well-defined trails. Distance is a variable factor in comparing routes along trails, paths, or bushwhacks.

Time is given as an additional gauge for the length of routes. This measure will give you a better understanding of the difficulty of the terrain, the change in elevation along the route, and the problems of finding a suitable course. Average pace for walking trails is 2 miles an hour, for paths, between 1½ and 2 miles an hour, and for bushwhacks, 1 mile an hour.

All the paths and trails described in this book can be hiked in one day. Some are very short, and some can be combined to make longer backpacking trips. A few of the lakes are sufficiently beautiful to warrant camping trips of several days' duration, and where this is possible, camping spots are described.

The *canoe trips,* like the walks, are gentle meanders on slow-moving streams. There is generally no safe whitewater canoeing in the area although both the East Canada Creek and West Branch of the Sacandaga have wild stretches. Many of the canoe trips pass through *flowed lands,* the ubiquitous, marshy, flooded areas of the upland plateaus. They result from the drying of glacial lakes, from silting and dying lakes, and from enterprising beaver.

The region's swamps and bogs were originally called *vlaies* by Dutch and German settlers. That name has been corrupted into the term *vly,* which natives of the southern Adirondacks further changed to *fly.* No matter what they are called, they make wet walking.

Many of the routes not only serve hikers in summer but also *snowshoers* and *cross-country skiers* in winter. As a result the revised guide also encourages winter use of the area. Those snowmobile trails that double as good cross-country ski routes are noted. Many bushwhacks are easiest in winter under a good snow cover, and those that are most suitable for snowshoe treks are so noted.

A surprising number of new routes and destinations have been discovered in the years since the guide was first published. There are probably many more. If you find new walks, please let me know so they may be included in future editions.

Each chapter in this revised guide contains a map or maps

showing all the routes and places mentioned in that chapter as accurately as possible. Each map is based on the USGS topographical sheet(s) appropriate to the area covered, as follows: Chapter 1, USGS 15' Piseco Lake, USGS 15' Lake Pleasant, USGS 7½' Stratford, and USGS 7½' Canada Lake; Chapter II, USGS 7½' Lassellsville, USGS 7½' Peck Lake, and USGS 7½' Canada Lake; Chapter III, USGS 7½' Canada Lake and USGS 7½' Caroga Lake; Chapter IV, USGS 7½' Stratford, USGS 7½' Canada Lake, and USGS 7½' Caroga Lake; Chapter V, USGS 7½' Stratford and USGS 7½' Canada Lake; Chapter VI, USGS 7½' Canada Lake and USGS 7½' Caroga Lake; Chapter VII, USGS 15' Piseco Lake, USGS 15' Lake Pleasant, USGS 7½' Canada Lake, and USGS 7½' Caroga Lake; Chapter VIII, USGS 15' Piseco Lake and USGS 15' Lake Pleasant; Chapter IX, USGS 15' Lake Pleasant, USGS 7½' Caroga Lake, and USGS 15' Jackson Summit; Chapter X, USGS 7½' Northville; Chapter XI, USGS 15' Piseco Lake and USGS 15' Lake Pleasant; Chapter XII, USGS 15' Lake Pleasant.

The USGS sheets can be purchased at most sporting goods stores or directly from the government by writing to: Branch of Distribution, U.S. Geological Survey, 1200 South Eads Street, Arlington, Virginia 22202.

On all maps, each circled number refers to the route or place identified in the section bearing the same number. The following cartographic symbols are used to distinguish different kinds of routes:

Path ━ · ━ · ━ ·
Marked footpath ━ ━ ━
Trail ━ ━ ━ ━
Bushwhack • • • • • • • •
Dirt road ━ · ━ · ━ · ━ ·
Canoe route ━━━━━━━

Woodsmanship and the Adirondack Forest Preserve

The area surrounding the West Branch of the Sacandaga is designated the Silver Lake Wilderness. In a *Wilderness Area* man should leave only his footprints. The *Wild Forest* lands that comprise the south and west portions encompassed in this guide deserve the same reverence.

Camping is permitted throughout public lands that are part of the Adirondack Forest Preserve with a few exceptions, which are noted in the text. You may camp overnight without a permit, but camping at one location for more than three consecutive nights requires a permit from a local New York State Forest Ranger. To locate the ranger for an area, consult the white pages in the local phone book under New York State Department of Environmental Conservation Forest Ranger.

Only dead and downed wood may be used for *campfires*. Build fires in designated fire rings or dig down to rock, sand, or gravel, below root level. Fire is dangerous and can travel rapidly through the duff or organic soil, burning roots and spreading along them. Douse your fires with water, and be sure they are completely out and cold before you leave. Burn all combustible trash, and carry out everything else. Carry a trash bag for your own use and to help clean up after thoughtless people who may have preceded you.

Most of the unusual *wildflowers* noted in the text are on the list of plants protected by law. Do not pick them or try to bring them home to transplant. All ferns, with the exception of bracken and hay-scented fern, are also protected.

Some of the routes in the guide traverse *private lands*. The text generally describes the means of obtaining permission to cross these properties. Never cross private lands without the owner's permission. Unless the text expressly identifies the area as state-owned Forest Preserve or private land whose owner permits unrestricted public passage, the inclusion of a route description does not imply public right-of-way.

Safety in the Woods

Never travel alone. Be sure someone knows your planned itinerary. A wide variety of navigational skills is required for the trails, paths, and bushwhacks described. Remember, you can get lost on any of the unmarked routes. The woods continually change. Blowdowns, fires, and new growth all alter the terrain. Do not attempt a route that is beyond your skill, but do try to improve your knowledge of the woods, for the rewards are great. The best destinations lie off the beaten path.

Use care near cliff tops! Even in the gentle terrain described in the guide a number of cliffs are potentially dangerous. All directions are for hikers who wish to find the safest way around the cliffs to their tops. Rock climbers could probably enjoy some of the cliffs, but this guide contains no technical rock climbing suggestions.

You will want to carry the appropriate USGS topographical

map of the area you are traveling, and you will want to know how to use it. A compass and the knowledge of its use are also essential. Your day pack should also contain a small first-aid kit, matches, raingear, and a canteen.

Besides a map and compass, I carry a small altimeter. Even though its accuracy is limited by changes in atmospheric pressure, it is an invaluable aid in bushwhacking mountains and finding cliffs. You may want to carry a small magnifying glass for examining plant and fern specimens and for resolving contour lines. I recommend wearing unbreakable glasses to protect your eyes. Almost none of the routes described are free of overhanging limbs and branches.

I

The Powley-Piseco Road and the East Canada Creek

The Powley-Piseco Road is a narrow dirt and gravel road for more than half its distance. Because it gives access to so many remote lakes and streams, it is a true wilderness passageway. It intersects Route 10 in the north, ¼ mile south of the bridge over the Big Bay of Piseco Lake. The village of Stratford and Route 29A are at the southern end of the road, 8⅔ miles west of Route 10 at Pine Lake. Along the entire nineteen miles in between, you can find the entrances to more walks and adventures than the road has miles.

Signs at the north end call this the Powley Road, after John C. Powley who tried to farm near the headwaters of the East Canada Creek sometime before 1880. At the southern end, signs designate it the Piseco Road, but for descriptive and romantic reasons, I prefer to use the double name.

It is not known exactly when in the nineteenth century the road was first used. It may date from before 1850. Even its twentieth-century history is vague. A few adventurous travelers remember driving along it in the late 1920s and early 1930s. The bridge over Brayhouse Brook, about a mile south of the halfway point, was washed out in the early 1940s, and the road was not open to cars throughout the rest of the 1940s and into the 1950s.

This romantic wilderness route remains so little known and used that it is amusing to contemplate the fate it almost suffered. In 1837, a survey was proposed for a railroad between Little Falls and Rackett (Raquette) Lake to run along the East Canada Creek, then north to Piseco's North Shore Road, and on north into the wilderness. It was one of the fantasies spun out from Albany to enhance the value of wilderness lands. Fortunately, the level route, almost the same route as the Powley-Piseco Road, was never developed.

In fact, until the last few years, the road was such a unique wilderness route that I often recommended it as a drive for friends who no longer hike. The surface of the northern part of the road remains dirt and unpaved, but during the late 1970s a program of widening the road disturbed the forest canopy that distinguished it as a wilderness route. Little more work will be done to widen the road, which can now accommodate two cars side by side, and trees are already beginning to arch over it again.

It is still possible to park almost anywhere along the road and enjoy a short walk and rarely be disturbed by the passage of another car. Bordered by mosses and ferns, it offers a reasonably dry place to tramp when other woods trails are too wet for hiking.

You should pay particular attention to directions for the paths north of the confluence of Brayhouse Brook and the East Canada: almost none of them are marked, and the sportsmen who use them are careful to keep the beginnings of some of them concealed. The recent work to widen and improve the old one-lane dirt road has resulted in many new turnouts that can easily be confused with the parking spots for some of the paths. The list of road distances at the end of this introduction to Chapter I should help those unfamiliar with the road and paths locate specific routes.

The road traverses a rather flat upland plateau with many shallow lakes and easy, though often wet, trails. In spite of the relatively flat terrain, the area contains some of the most beautiful places covered in this guide.

Several rift valleys, which lie in a northwest to southeast direction, border the road, and one, near Clockmill Corners, is especially lovely. The valleys developed through erosion in the ancient pre-Cambrian rock base, following the fault lines in that basic metamorphic rock.

The large grassy meadows and sand flats at Powley Place, south of Clockmill Corners, give evidence of the glacial lake that covered all of that area. As the lake receded, glacial sand deposits filled the valley. Later the upper reaches of the East Canada Creek cut through the flats, giving the stream its softly eroded banks.

There is relatively little difference in elevation between many of the lakes that drain to form the East Canada, and most unusual is the fact that within recent times several have had their outlet directions change. One, Ferris Lake, has two different outlets, both of which eventually make their way to the East Canada Creek.

All of the streams and lakes south of Clockmill Corners flow into the East Canada, and the Powley-Piseco Road follows the creek's valley for much of its distance. Not only is there surprisingly little change in elevation along the valley floor, but the mountains only rise a few hundred feet above it. In spite of this, there are some lovely hills. One of the prettiest sections is the valley between East Notch and West Notch mountains. Walking along the road between the Notch Mountains is the best way to appreciate the cliffs on West Notch Mountain that face the road.

There are several attractive picnic spots along the road or near it, many of which are used by campers. Some of the best are described in section 19. All are on state land and camping is allowed (see Introduction).

Among the picnic spots beside the East Canada, a few are so special as to rival any in the Adirondacks. It is remarkable how secluded you can feel in these quiet nooks and how obvious it is that the unpaved road is responsible for it.

Almost all of the northern two-thirds of the road is in the Forest Preserve; the one big exception is the area called Oregon, where there used to be a dam on the East Canada Creek. The unpaved part of the road, from Oregon to Route 10, is not plowed in winter; snowmobilers use it and may of the trails radiating from it. Therefore, consider trails in the north as destinations for spring, summer, and fall outings.

In the south, from Route 29A north to Oregon, most of the land on either side of the road is private. You are introduced to the delights that border this part of the Powley-Piseco Road with three exceptions to that generalization. Sections 1, 2 and 3 are special short walks on small parcels of Forest Preserve land.

Mileages to and along the Powley-Piseco Road, from south to north

Miles	Section number	Place
0.0	—	Stratford; Route 29A, Mike Smith Road, and County Route 104 intersect
0.2	—	Mike Smith Road intersects the Powley-Piseco Road
2.5	—	Powley-Piseco Road reaches dirt road marked dead-end

+0.1	1	Dirt road passes Mussey Dam (side trip)
+0.5	2	Dirt road reaches iron bridge (side trip)
4.3	—	Powley-Piseco Road reaches Seeley Road extension on east
4.5	—	Powley-Piseco Road crosses old iron bridge over North Creek
4.6	—	Powley-Piseco Road crosses new bridge over North Creek
6.4	—	Powley-Piseco Road crosses bridge at Oregon
7.0	3	Powley-Piseco Road reaches path on west to House Pond
8.0	4	Powley-Piseco Road reaches dirt road on west along Brayhouse Gore
8.3	5	Powley-Piseco Road reaches The Potholers and new culvert bridge over Brayhouse Brook
9.7	6	Powley-Piseco Road reaches parking for path to Brayhouse Brook
11.0	7-9	Powley-Piseco Road reaches Powley Place bridge over the East Canada Creek and trailhead for route to Big Alderbed
11.5	10	Powley-Piseco Road reaches road to Ferris Lake on east
12.7	11	Powley-Piseco Road reaches parking for path to Goldmine Stream
14.6	12	Powley-Piseco Road passes cairn marking bushwhack route to Christian Lake
14.9	13-17	Powley-Piseco Road reaches Clockmill Corners
15.5	18	Powley-Piseco Road reaches Mud Pond
16.3	19	Powley-Piseco Road passes camping spot on west
17.1	20-21	Powley-Piseco Road passes

1 Mussey Dam
Short path; walking, picnicking, swimming, fishing

Many lovely picnic places line the East Canada Creek. One is called Mussey Dam by the natives, and there may at one time have been a dam nearby. However, nothing of it remains, and there is no one left who remembers if there every really was one.

In this wild and beautifully rocky stretch of the creek you will enjoy good views both upstream and down. Here the granite faces of the shores funnel the tumultuous stream through a steep, narrow sluice into a deep pool, which is suitable for both swimming and fishing. Adventurous youngsters may even enjoy shooting the sluice into the pool below.

To reach the spot, drive on the Powley-Piseco Road for 2½ miles north of Stratford to a dirt road on the left, or west, which is marked only "dead end." Drive west on the road for 1/10 mile, where it bends sharply right. Here there is room to park off the road. To the left, a dirt road that is not suitable for vehicles heads south and west toward the East Canada, ⅛ mile away. Walk along it and then the continuing path to the creek and the picnic spot. You should reach it in five minutes.

2 The Abandoned Farm
Path along old road; walking, picnicking, fishing

The dirt road described in section 1 continues for a total of ½ mile from the Powley-Piseco Road to an old iron bridge over the East Canada. The stream and its banks north of the bridge are posted, but land to the south and west is not. Cross the bridge and walk up the old farm road toward the high meadows on the west.

The road heads northwest and then angles southwest, through a forested area to reach fields with many wildflowers, raspberries, and blueberries. The abandoned farm is a good example of the ways the forest begins to reclaim land. The road continues a little north of west up the hill. Near the crest, the deep mosses in the open fields provide a beautiful rug for a picnic, and the spot is high enough to attract a fresh breeze and permit distant mountain views.

The crest is so barren of grasses and shrubs that it is certain the underlying hills are sterile banks of sand, perhaps washed from the great glacial lake that filled the East Canada Valley. Similar sterile banks and fields can be seen in many places from the Powley-Piseco Road.

The unposted water south of the bridge is supposed to have good fishing, and in any event, this part of the creek is delightful. A small island divides the creek downstream of the bridge. You will enjoy both the area of the bridge and the fields to the west as places to sit and watch for birds and butterflies. Or you can lie in the deep mosses on the crest and simply watch passing clouds.

3 House Pond
Short path along old road; walking

Just short of 7 miles north of Stratford there is a parking place on the west side of the Powley-Piseco Road, opposite Oregon Mountain. A path beginning at the turnout leads a little over ½ mile to House Pond. An easy twenty-minute walk will take you to this small pond, which is shown more accurately on older USGS maps than on the most recent issue. Because it is now, as it was during the 1901 USGS survey, mostly a swampy lake, it will probably become a dry lake in the not-too-distant future, unless an active beaver can raise the water level to the height shown on the 1954 USGS map.

House Pond's eastern shore has a dry slope covered with spruce and hemlock, and there is open water at its northern end. On the south, much of it is open swamp, with a pretty evergreen-covered peninsula separating the two halves.

Although the path to the pond is fairly easy to follow, there is one confusing fork about three minutes' walking time (200 yards) from the road. The path on the left goes on to the lake; the one on the right seems to follow an old logging road that winds generally northward and disappears entirely after swinging back toward the road.

This is a gentle walk, and though House Pond is not among the prettiest of little ponds, it is fascinating for the way it shows how woods plants invade a dying lake.

The East Canada Creek

4 Brayhouse Gore
Path along old road; walking

One-quarter mile south of the bridge over Brayhouse Brook, a dirt road heads west from the Powley-Piseco Road toward a camp. The history of the road is fascinating; it wanders through a narrow strip of land called the Brayhouse Gore, which lies on the border of Fulton and Hamilton counties.

In successive surveys in 1768 by Isaac Vrooman and 1794 by Simeon De Witt, two different points were established for the western end of the line that separated the Jerseyfield Patent and the Lawrence Tract. Later surveys produced two more points. It was not until 1883 that Verplank Colvin determined the correct boundary, adding considerable lands to the state holdings. The Gore was placed in Hamilton County, but not before a road had been built through the disputed lands that private interests claimed.

Today the road begins on private but unposted land and leads an easy 2 miles northwest to a cabin. Land past the cabin is part of the Forest Preserve. The road ends just north of a large vly, where an ill-defined path continues northwest toward Black Creek Lake and the road past Jerseyfield.

5 The Potholers
Short path; walking, picnicking, camping

Probably the most beautiful of all the picnic places in the southern Adirondacks, the Potholers was named by children who enjoy the individual bathtubs, or potholes, which have been worn in the granite stream bed by rocks churned in the waters of the East Canada Creek. The creek is often gentle in summer, but it can be a raging torrent in wet weather.

There is parking along the Powley-Piseco Road both north and south of the bridge over Brayhouse Brook. The charming old iron bridge gave way in the spring floods of 1977 and has been recently replaced by a large, nondescript culvert.

On the north side of the bridge, walk east for 100 feet along the Brayhouse to a lovely but well-used campsite overlooking the

The East Canada Creek near the confluence with Brayhouse Brook

East Canada Creek. Continue along the creek on one of the several unmarked paths. The Potholers is a five-minute walk upstream.

The East Canada from the Brayhouse confluence upstream to the still water above the Potholers is a series of small waterfalls and many rock slides, making it one of the Adirondacks' most photogenic waterfall areas.

In July, the small meadow north of the campsite bursts forth in one of the most spectacular displays of native wildflowers in the entire Forest Preserve. Often more than a hundred purple-fringed orchis, with spikes two- to three-feet tall, bear a myriad of delicate little orchid-shaped flowers. Please, do not pick or touch the plants. One of the paths to the Potholers passes right through the meadow, and it is a miracle that these flowers have survived and multiplied with so much traffic. If you are observant, walking these paths will also introduce you to the great variety of mosses and ferns and ground-cover plants that grace the north woods.

The paths all lead to a flat rock projecting into the stream with still water above and a series of rapids and falls below. There is one waterfall under which youngsters delight in hiding, water conditions permitting. My children also enjoyed shooting the rapids in inner tubes and tiny plastic boats.

The upper rock is ideal for a cookout and is almost always kept free of bugs by a fresh breeze. Framed by the deep moist woods on either side, the rushing stream with its noisy cataracts is an exquisitely beautiful place.

6 Brayhouse Brook
Short path; walking, picnicking, fishing

Among the many fishermen's paths that are gems to explore, the one along Brayhouse Brook is especially inviting; but like most of these paths, the beginning is unfortunately well concealed. The path is to the west of the Powley-Piseco Road and begins in a marshy depression about 75 yards north of a parking spot on the east side of the road 9⅔ miles north of Stratford. The path's entrance would probably escape all notice if you were not really looking for it, and road work has made it more difficult to spot than ever. You may have to walk along the road to find it.

Once found, the path is easy to follow for ½ mile across the high ground of the shoulder of Sugarbush Mountain to a ledge that is about 20 feet above Brayhouse Brook. The steep bank, covered with hemlocks and shielding the lovely brook below, is a charming discovery. The ledge is rimmed with ferns and mosses as are the stream banks below.

A path drops to stream level, continues on the north bank into a swampy area, and disappears. Fishermen and hunters tell that some trail from this area continues west along the brook to the southern end of Long Lake and on to Diamond Lake, but I could find no real path and I suspect that there is none suitable for casual hikers. This is certainly an area where it would be desirable to have a worn path, for the remote mountains surrounding the stream are lovely to explore, and there is no other route from the east to those lakes.

7 Big Alderbed
Trail; hiking, fishing, camping

The old logging road to Big Alderbed has been marked as a snowmobile trail. There is evidence that other motorized vehicles have illegally used the road in recent years, but that should not deter hikers. The road provides a lovely, long walk, and it leads to beautiful places, among them Big Alderbed itself, its outlet (which is the beginning of the West Branch of the East Canada Creek), and an exceptionally pretty grassy vly through which the outlet flows.

The trail begins from a parking spot on the Powley-Piseco Road just south of the Powley Place bridge over the West Branch of the East Canada. The bridge is 11 miles north of Stratford.

The trail brings you to a small stream after a half-hour's walk, a second stream a half-hour later, and finally, a half-hour beyond that, to a beautiful stretch of the Big Alderbed outlet stream. The 2½-mile walk to this spot is easy, over relatively flat terrain.

In low water, crossing the stream is just a matter of hopping rocks, but spring meltwater and autumn rains can make crossing then impossible — as the presence of a cable and a hand car indicate.

It is less than ½ mile from the crossing to the dam at the outlet of Big Alderbed, a section in which the trail climbs along as lovely a stretch of wild stream as there is in the area. Because the trail is just out of sight of the stream bed, you might wish to follow closer to the stream here. Try this as a spring walk, when the beauty of the falls is enhanced by the spring floods.

The dam at the end of Big Alderbed is a high one, constructed of a wooden crib filled with large stones. It appears to have been four feet higher at one time than it is now. As it is, the level of the lake is higher than the remains of the dam would otherwise make it because of the addition of a beaver dam on top of the manmade structure. There are several large, old beaver houses in the lake. The shores of the lake have been stripped of small trees so that parts of them are quite open, with numerous beaver slides along the steep banks.

Big Alderbed's entire northern end is very shallow and filled with weeds and stumps, and parts are only mud flats. You will find an amazing number of ducks on the lake in August. Even with the low water and despite the fact that it is partly manmade, Big Alderbed is a pretty lake with high hills on both the north and south.

Sportsmen have made paths from the area of the lake south toward Long Lake and north toward Trout Lake, but I have found no really usable hiking paths. Obviously, many sportsmen use the region, and with good reason, for the cleared banks provided by the beavers make good graze areas for deer, and many signs of deer are to be found.

There is a good, dry campsite at the east end of the lake, and a fine place for picnicking or fishing.

I had the opportunity to walk this trail twice in one season, once in early July and again in late August; the difference was remarkable. Needless to say, the trail was much drier the second time, but there were other more dramatic changes. Although the forest along the trail is composed of mixed hardwoods, with some trees of very good size, as in other areas there is a preponderance of mature beech. The recent beech die-back has caused several trees to fall across the trail, and in places the downing of beech has been so severe as to leave large openings in the forest. Here more light reaches the forest floor, encouraging the heavy growth of witch hobble and other plants. The marked change in just one summer on this trail is undoubtedly reflected in all the paths of the region, and it is possible that many will become less easy to follow in the next few years.

The round-trip walk to the lake is just short of 6 miles long and requires three and a half hours.

8 West Branch of the East Canada Creek
Easy bushwhack

East of the point where the snowmobile trail to Big Alderbed (section 7) crosses the West Branch, there is, barely visible in heavy underbrush, the remnant of another logging road. This one follows the West Branch downstream and makes a pleasant alternate return route from the Big Alderbed lake.

While it is not easy to follow the old road, it is easy to proceed here if you bushwhack, following the south side of the stream. The walking is very difficult, but worthwhile, for after a half-hour's trek you reach a lovely open meadow framed by the spruce of Big Alderbed Mountain. Another half-hour suffices to walk through the meadow to its eastern end, where there are several short paths, all used by hunters and leading to nearby campsites (some of which are even equipped with well-rusted iron stoves). From the southern end of the meadow, a bushwhack due south for 200 yards brings you back to the snowmobile trail.

The very wildness of the woods and the remoteness of the meadow make it hard to believe that all its fall visitors (hunters) are so numerous, but the quiet beauty of this place in summer makes it a lovely area to explore.

9 East Canada Creek/Northern Flow
Canoe Trip

If the West Branch of the Sacandaga (section 58) is the king of canoe trips in this region, certainly the prince is the northern-most flow of the East Canada. It is extremely accessible, since the Powley-Piseco Road crosses the flow by the Powley Place bridge. North and west of the bridge stretches a large meadow that was once farmland. The farm has long since disappeared, but its name survives.

It takes only a short canoe trip to explore the still waters of the flow, but for absolute peace in a remote area, the creek has few rivals. You can easily spend two hours exploring the flows on each side of the bridge, so adventures in both directions can stretch an outing to more than a half-day.

Canoeing west of the bridge over several small beaver dams for a distance of about ½ mile, you will find the creek choked with alders. Recent beaver work has flooded the stretch upstream, so if you can get through the dense alders here, you will have another mile or more of canoeable water through the meadows just east of Big Alderbed. This section of the trip west of the bridge is dependent on beaver flows and water levels, however.

The still water east of the bridge stretches over 1½ miles and is canoeable even in midsummer when the water is low. At that time there are many sights and sounds to delight.

Sugarbush Mountain, west of the creek, dominates most of the view from the water on the eastern portion of the trip, and the magnificent stands of enormous spruce are especially lovely. The cool shade they provide and their splendid reflections in the still, deep water, occasionally highlighted with the reflected white clusters of elderberry blossoms, make this a painter's delight. Blooming meadowsweet against the blue-green of sweetgale provides a contrast to the gently waving grasses and their graceful cascades over the stream banks. Alders, viburnum, and royal fern fill out the shoreline of this typical quiet upland stream.

You will be amused by the appearance of huge green frogs, sunning along the muddy banks or floating on the weed beds. Their many shades of green more than rival the greens of the plants along the banks.

For most of the distance on the east side of the bridge, the creek flows in a north-south direction, paralleling the Powley-Piseco Road but sufficiently far from it that no road sounds intrude. The trip is a very easy and leisurely wilderness experience.

10 Ferris Lake
Dirt road; walking, canoeing

A dirt road over private lands connects the Powley-Piseco Road and Ferris Lake. The mile-long road begins at the northern end of the meadows at the Powley Place, on the east side of Powley-Piseco Road, just under 11½ miles north of Stratford.

Walking is permitted along the road to Ferris Lake, though its owners do *not* want anyone to drive on it. Please respect their wishes. Camping is also not allowed on the private lands near the road. The use of good judgment in this situation will help keep all such places open to the public. While a short stretch of the shore near the road is also private, the lake is not.

The lake is almost a mile long, with a charming island and dense spruce-covered shores. It is an especially fine lake to explore in a canoe, and in spite of the small cluster of cabins near the road it is quiet and isolated.

Just remember, the road and lands near it are private, and no camping is allowed.

11 Goldmine Stream
Short path; walking, picnicking, fishing

Many of the paths in the Southern Adirondacks used by hunters and fishermen lead to especially beautiful and almost unknown spots. One of the prettiest is the waterfall area on Goldmine Stream.

Two paths start in to Goldmine Stream, both about 1¾ miles north of Powley Place bridge on the Powley-Piseco Road. Look on the east side of the road for a parking spot, which road construction constantly changes. Some 100 yards north on the opposite (west) side of the road, you may spot one of the paths. Because the entrances to both are not only unmarked but almost invisible, they may be difficult to locate. Simply walk along the west side of the road in the general vicinity until you spot one. Within 100 feet of the road, both paths become very obvious and by the time they join as they cross a small stream, between 200 and 300 yards west of the road, the route is easy to follow. With the exceptions of one area just before the stream and others in the vicinity of several blowdowns, the path shows a good amount of use as it continues due west.

Just over ½ mile from the start, a half-hour's walk at most, the path forks. The left branch descends 200 yards to a hunting camp where the outlet of Christian Lake flows into Goldmine Stream. There is even a rickety suspension bridge over Goldmine Stream here.

Above the camp, the stream is flat and makes a large bend to the south. The right fork bypasses that bend and the pools in the stream with their swampy borders. After crossing the outlet of Christian Lake, it proceeds just south of west over high ground to the area of rapids and falls on Goldmine Stream. The path here is difficult to follow in several places, sometimes because of blowdowns and in two or three small meadows because heavy fern growth obscures the route.

Even with these cautions, it is no more than a twenty-minute walk from the fork to one of the prettiest small streams flowing into the East Canada. Total walking time from the road rarely exceeds forty-five minutes.

Rapids and little falls extend for nearly ¼ mile. At the western end of the rapids a broad shimmer of water drops twelve feet over a smooth golden granite outcrop into a deep trout pool. Farther upstream the water flows over a relatively smooth rocky bed. You can explore the stream here by following a fishermen's footpath until it gradually peters out.

Because there are many perfect picnic rocks as well as many quiet scenes to view, you will be well rewarded on this short walk to a wild and remote stream.

A word of caution: The footpath is as difficult to retrace as it is to find. You should make mental note of the confusing places on the walk in to the falls to help you on the return.

12 Christian Lake
Easy bushwhack; fishing,
camping, picnicking

The route to Christian Lake illustrates perfectly the ways in which the forest continually changes. In 1973 searching for the sportsmen's informal path to Christian Lake was almost futile. Blowdowns from the beech die-back totally obscured the route. Today the tops of the downed beeches are fast disappearing, and the path is relatively obvious.

The path follows a draw on the north shoulder of West Notch Mountain. Its beginning is on the west side of the Powley-Piseco Road within sight and 200 yards north of the cliffs on that mountain. Watch for the rocky bed of an intermittent stream; a small rock cairn beside it marks the start of the path. It climbs steeply for 300 yards and then more gradually as it enters a saddle bordered on both sides by small rock ledges and cliffs. The path continues through the saddle but does not descend to the lake through the obvious draw at its western end. There, before descending, look for several blazes and red markers on trees on your right. The path climbs out of the draw and heads downhill toward the flows at the northern end of Christian Lake. Below the saddle the route is almost due west. Blazes and paint daubs help define the faint path.

After descending to the level of the lake, the path crosses two streams in a wet, wooded meadow, with sphagnum underfoot and hemlock above. Continue west for 50 feet, and then swing south to the west shore of the lake, where there are several campsites. The heavily wooded slopes of West Notch Mountain rise above the deep, clear lake on the opposite shore. This remote, wilderness destination can be reached within forty-five minutes.

However, this is an unmarked path, and it is not always clear, so only attempt it if you feel comfortable using a map and compass. One section of the return can present more problems than any part of the trip in. After leaving the lake, walk north to the wet area, cross it to the hillside on the west, and look for the short, steep draw you'll climb to return. At present, this draw is identified by unofficial orange markers. *Be sure you pick the proper draw.* A second one, beginning less than 100 feet north of the desired one, leads from the meadow northeast to an impenetrable spruce swamp. It is easy to become confused.

13 Clockmill Corners to Kennels Pond
Trail along old road;
hiking, cross-country skiing

The most beautiful snowmobile trail in this area for hikers heads southeast from Clockmill Corners, a remote bend in the Powley-Piseco Road almost 15 miles north of Stratford. There is nothing at this valley junction to indicate why or how it received its romantic name.

There are several reasons why hikers find this trail so desirable. For one, it is not freshly cut, but rather follows an old logging road. It also runs down a rift valley, permitting exploration of the valley and its lakes and ponds, as well as allowing access to several other interior ponds and small valleys. The snowmobile trails extend east to the private lands surrounding Kennels Pond (section 70), just off Route 10.

There are two good ways to enjoy the walk through the valley. Either hike the 3½-mile distance southeast from Clockmill Corners to the abandoned beaver meadow known as Teeter Creek Vly and return the same way to your car, or arrange to make a one-way trek the full length of the valley — a distance of 4½ miles — with transportation at each end. If you wish to make the one-way trip, ask permission of one of the agents of Robert Avery, who owns the land around Kennels Pond. You will find them in one of the houses on Route 10 between Avery's Hotel (now closed) and the pond. Hikers may cross the land as long as they do not carry fishing poles or firearms. Since the land along the south side of Kennels Pond has recently been logged, the mile of road between Teeter Creek Vly and Route 10 is not now the prettiest of walking routes.

There is only a 75-foot drop in elevation from the Powley-Piseco Road to Kennels Pond, so the trail, which keeps to high ground through the valley, is quite flat and easy. It is possible to make the 4½-mile trip through the valley in not much over two hours, except that there are so many lovely diversions along the way. So, no matter whether you choose the round-trip trek or the one-way hike, or plan side excursions or not, you should give yourself a whole day's outing for this adventure.

The surrounding forests of good-sized and fairly old hardwoods add to the pleasure of the walk. Some of the trees that have succumbed to old age are over three feet in diameter. The trail passes a number of small brooks that flow into the larger streams in the valley, and there are several lovely small ferny meadows along the way.

Most attractive are the lakes and vlies along the valley or accessible from it. Just southeast of Clockmill Corners, the trail skirts a handsome swampy meadow that appears to have a natural dike across its small outlet. This dike is visible ⅓ mile from the Powley-Piseco Road on the north side of the trail. After ½ mile the little stream turns west to join the outlet of Mud Lake, and the swamplands there are barely visible from the trail.

The trail forks in a weed-filled, open meadow 1¼ miles from the Powley-Piseco Road. Markings here are poor. The left fork heads toward Clockmill Pond (section 14); the right fork follows the long axis of the meadow to the southeast before entering the woods again on a relatively discernible track marked with only one or two of the large DEC yellow-orange snowmobile trail markers.

The trail skirts just south of a small, unnamed shallow pond ¼ mile past the fork. The pond's outlet flows southeast through the valley, paralleling the trail, to Rock Lake, which is ½ mile away. Rock Lake is ⅓ mile long, and because the trail is high on its steep southern bank, you only catch glimpses of its rocky shores through the trees. You will want to leave the trail to see the lake.

A mile south of Rock Lake and within ¼ mile of Kennels Pond, the trail skirts the southern end of my favorite, picturesque, grassy vly. Called Teeter Creek Vly by natives, it extends more than ¼ mile to the northwest.

The snowmobile trail leaves the old logging road in the area of the vly in order to avoid crossing it. Swinging northwest of the vly, it follows the west side on high and dry ground. The northern extension of the trail then circles around the south of Matts Mountain, crosses Teeter Creek and one of its tributaries, and then heads northeast toward the parking turnout on Route 10 (section 71). From the parking turnout north, the snowmobile route generally parallels Route 10 to the Sand Lake outlet, which it crosses on a good new bridge before finally intersecting the Powley-Piseco Road. The trail then continues along the Powley-Piseco Road, past Sand Lake, back to Clockmill Corners. While the northern extension holds little interest for hikers, it completes the loop for a superior 13-mile-long snowmobile trip.

The redesigned trail in the vicinity of the Teeter Creek Vly keeps snowmobiles from the swamps, but it does not help hikers who have obtained permission to cross the posted land and wish to continue straight to Kennels Pond. Circle the south end of the vly on dry ground and opposite the trail's first approach to the vly, about 200 yards across it, climb the south slope beside the meadow to find the path again. It continues through a hemlock stand to Kennels Pond. The head of this pond is remote and lovely, giving no indication of the roads and building hidden on the Route 10 end.

The 7-mile round-trip between Clockmill Corners and the head of Kennels Pond can be walked in four hours. You will want to allow much more time, either to explore the sights mentioned above or to make the excursions from the trail outlined in the next three sections.

Because the Powley-Piseco Road is unplowed, those who wish to ski this route should, with permission, start their trip from the Route 10 end, using the new ski trails marked out around Kennels Pond (see section 70).

14 Clockmill Pond

Path on old road; walking, canoeing,
fishing, picnicking, camping

Clockmill Pond is only ½ mile from the fork in the Clockmill Corners snowmobile trail described in section 13. It is so close to both the trail and the Powley-Piseco Road that it makes either a great short walk or a pleasant diversion on the longer trek to Kennels Pond.

As noted in section 13, the snowmobile trail emerges in a small, grassy meadow 1¼ miles from the Powley-Piseco Road, with the trail forking to the right. The old road to Clockmill Pond forks from

Near Clockmill Pond

the left side of the meadow, less than 50 yards around its eastern end. In the weeks of mid-summer, the point where the old road leaves the meadow may be concealed, but once you find the roadway the path along it will be quite obvious.

The path is unmarked and leads to the pond's northwest side and then along a promontory to its outlet, where a manmade rock dam was added to the natural dike. The lake is extremely pretty, although the water's warmth indicates it is not deep. Huge exposed rocks line the southern shore, a lovely spruce-covered island seems to float in the middle of the pond, and many water lilies fill the shallows.

A mill did occupy a site near the outlet, but little of it remains. All you will find is a large wheel and gear lying just below the beaver dam that crowns the manmade structure. No historical record has yet been found of the mill or its purpose. All that is known is that it may have existed before the middle of the nineteenth century.

Either carry a canoe to the pond or use an inflatable boat, for the many bays along the ½-mile stretch of water are fun to explore. The inlet stream is canoeable through flowed lands for over ½ mile toward Rock Lake. Excellent camping spots can be found along the pond's shores, some near the outlet. Perhaps the best is on the rocky southern shore most easily reached by boat.

This path is among my favorite fall walks. Mid- to late September finds the swamp maples around the pond aflame with dark reds. Camera buffs might delight in the reflections in the tiny pool just below the outlet. A beaver dam at the outlet of the shallow pond just below Clockmill Pond has washed away recently, and that small pond is already giving way to new meadows full of lush, tall grasses.

15 Black Cat Lake
Easy bushwhack; hiking,
fishing, camping

After following the Clockmill Corners snowmobile trail (section 13) almost halfway along the shore of Rock Lake, a total distance of nearly 2 miles from the Powley-Piseco Road, you will cross a small inlet stream. Seventy-five yards to its east, it is possible, with a vivid imagination, to discern an old logging road on your right. This road follows a small valley between two hills for ¾ mile west-southwest to Black Cat Lake. The road can be followed to

Black Cat Lake, but whether by advanced path finding or bush-whacking is difficult to decide.

It is essential to have a contour map and compass for this walk. The road climbs a small draw, crosses the height-of-land, and descends another draw to the lake. In the draw on the east side of the ridge, the road bed is to the south of a marshy area and can be followed except in two places. The path fades near the top, then becomes obvious again after passing through a small (thirty-foot-diameter) meadow. Descending the west side, it generally follows a dry stream bed into the valley, this time staying to the north of the draw. All signs of the road seem to disappear in the heavy growth of the wet southeastern shores of Black Cat Lake.

I wonder what event prompted the naming of the lake, which is a charming area with a beaver dam and house near the outlet and a dark, evergreen-covered shoreline. Fishermen frequent the lake, and there are signs of campers. Allowing forty-five minutes for the easy bushwhack from the trail, the pond can be reached in two hours from Clockmill Corners.

16 Iron Lake
Bushwhack; hiking, snowshoeing, fishing

An old road heads almost due west from the logging road that follows the south shore of Kennels Pond, at a point 300 yards north of the pond (see section 13). The old road starts on private land and ends by Iron Lake, which is on state land. As a bush-whack route, the road bed is even less easy to follow than the one to Black Cat Lake (section 15), so you would be better advised simply to follow the small stream that flows ¼ mile from a swampy area between Kennels Pond and Iron Lake. From the swampy area it is another ¼-mile-long bushwhack due west to the lake. It is too bad that there are no real trails here, because Iron Lake is lovely, with steep shores and rocky outcrops heavily covered with evergreen forests. However, even walking the shores of the lake is difficult, if not impossible.

The trek to Iron Lake via this route should take no more than an hour from the logging road, or three hours from Clockmill Corners. It can also be reached from Route 10, and with permission, the latter is the recommended approach in winter for snowshoers.

It is also possible to reach this lake from Jockeybush Lake (section 69). Some people have walked the outlet of Black Cat on snowshoes to the outlet of Iron Lake and thence upstream to

45

the lake itself. I tried this approach in summer, but the heavy growth of evergreens makes some areas impenetrable.

17 Mud Pond
Path; walking

There are actually twenty Mud Ponds and six Mud Lakes within the Blue Line of the Adirondack Park. You might be tempted to fault the lack of imagination on the part of early map makers, but you will not be able to find any pond so named that is not muddy. This one has a lovely bog to explore and is so close to the Powley-Piseco Road that getting to it can scarcely be called a short walk. The pond lies east of the road and is visible from it. The parking spot at the beginning of the path is 15½ miles north of Stratford. Look for the pond through the trees on the south side of the road and a little over ½ mile beyond Clockmill Corners.

The flora is typical of a quaking bog. Cranberries and even wild calla are to be found. For those who enjoy the special plants that adapt to life in a bog, this is one of the three best bogs and among the most accessible of all those covered in this book. See Chub Lake (section 61), for details on the variety of bog plants you can expect.

18 Picnic and Camping Spots along the Powley-Piseco Road

As you drive north on the Powley-Piseco Road, you may notice several turnouts that are not mentioned in the list of trailheads or path beginnings. Most of these have been used by campers. Some spots are more handsome than others, and a few are worth considering if you wish to stay relatively close to the road. You can camp at any one for up to three days without a permit (see Introduction), and while they are often used on weekends, they are usually empty weekdays. Those noted below are especially desirable for their accessibility to the region's walks and canoe trips.

There are several campsites in the sand flats beside the road just north of the Powley Place bridge. These were created when the road was reconstructed, when sand was removed from the bed of the dry glacial lake that underlies the lovely meadow north of the bridge.

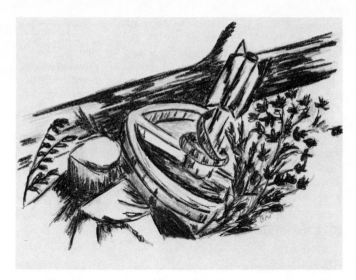

Wheel at Clockmill Pond

The three turnouts opposite Sugarbush Mountain, to the west of the Powley-Piseco Road between the parking turnout for the Brayhouse Brook path and the Powley Place bridge, can all be used for camping. Short paths lead from each to the East Canada Creek.

The northernmost, and probably the prettiest, of the camping spots lies at the end of a short dirt road heading west from the Powley-Piseco Road just under 1 mile north of the path to Mud Pond (section 17) and 16⅓ miles north of Stratford. The road leads less than 100 yards to a site beside a tiny stream that cuts through a deep sand bank. To the north the stream flows into a lovely grassy swamp that supports a profusion of turtlehead and purple asters in mid-August.

19 Sand Lake

Path; walking, canoeing, fishing,
camping, swimming

The Sand Lake path begins on the east side of the Powley-Piseco Road, exactly 2 miles from its northern end. It is an easy walk of about ⅓ mile although the middle section passes through a muddy wet area, which makes carrying a canoe difficult. Nevertheless, you should carry a canoe to the lake, for it is too pretty to just walk to, and there are no paths around the shores.

There is a campsite at the end of the path, which brings you to the outlet end of the lake. The eastern shore is sandy in places and good for swimming. With the shape of a fat *C* that arcs almost a mile, Sand Lake is one of the larger uninhabited lakes in the region.

Two enormous beaver houses marking the inlet end of the lake add to the interest of exploring by boat. With such a short walk, this lake is most desirable as a boating lake or a camping destination.

20 Clockmill Pond via Sand Lake
Canoe Trip

There are several hard carries in the canoe trip to Clockmill Pond, so many that at times it seems that there is more portaging than paddling. If you do not mind that and wet feet, this is a challenging and beautiful trip to an area visited today by only a few hunters.

After parking at the Sand Lake path entrance on the Powley-Piseco Road (section 19) and carrying the canoe to Sand Lake, paddle ¾ mile almost due south to the lake's inlet. There you will face a difficult 100-yard-carry up the rocky stream.

Above the carry, though, the stream is open and flat, coursing through flowed lands punctuated by a couple of small beaver dams that require portages. Even in low water this section is navigable, and with little current and much to see, it is easily accomplished. In fact the small beaver dams only assure that there is enough water at least for a bit more canoeing.

Another carry over a rocky section marks the end of the flowed lands. Just beyond, a very narrow stream enters the main channel from the south. The main channel is canoeable for a short way and in high water can be used to enter Mud Lake, so that if the shores of Mud Lake were anything but swamp you could put the canoe in there, and thus have a shorter carry from the road.

The side stream to the south is canoeable only a short distance. You will have to make a short (about ⅛ mile) portage on high ground northwest of the stream to a small unnamed pond to

Between Sand Lake and Clockmill Pond

continue to Clockmill Pond. The portage through the high hemlock woods along the stream, which has several little waterfalls, is not difficult. The unnamed pond has become noticeably smaller in the years between the first and second editions of this guide, but a channel threading through grassy fields is still navigable to within 200 yards of the Clockmill Pond dam.

The extra effort to carry the canoe the short distance from the unnamed pond to Clockmill Pond provides the chance to explore the southern rocky shore and the evergreen-covered island, as well as the navigable ½-mile stretch of inlet in the flowed lands to its southeast.

It is interesting to note that over the entire trip from Sand Lake to Clockmill Pond the elevation increases but 31 feet.

Walking and paddling, you will probably cover no more than 8 miles, but nearly seven hours are required for the trip, which must include a reviving swim on the return to Sand Lake. This outing is best done on a cool, breezy day, and the canoeing has to be classified as difficult because of the portages. But the remoteness of the whole adventure makes it a very special one-day trip.

21 Sheriff, Indigo and Jones Lakes

Trails, old logging roads; snowshoeing, cross-country skiing, hiking

On the west side of the Powley-Piseco Road, nearly opposite the start of the Clockmill Corners snowmobile trail, another snowmobile trail heads generally toward magnetic north through a draw and beside a series of wet meadows, eventually connecting with logging roads west of Sheriff Lake. The trailhead is 100 yards northeast of the Clockmill Corners trailhead and on the north side of a small stream. The route was cut to hook up the complex of trails in the Powley-Piseco Road area with the old roads between Sheriff Lake and Indigo and Jones lakes, which have accesses from Route 8 on the north.

The Sheriff Lake property and the woods around Indigo and Jones lakes, to its west, were heavily lumbered in the late 1970s. As a result, old roads and signposts have been obliterated, making it difficult to navigate in this area. Fortunately the shores of the lakes have not been touched, so things look normal and natural from the water. As of this writing, the property around

Sheriff Lake is for sale, and there is the possibility it will be acquired by the state.

So confusing are the logging roads in summer that hikers wanting to visit the lakes are really better advised not to use the snowmobile trail access from Clockmill Corners. Instead, drive west from Piseco on Route 8 and approach them from the north. In winter, because the Powley-Piseco Road is unplowed, the northern accesses are the only choices open to skiers and snowshoers.

To reach Indigo and Jones lakes from Route 8, find the snow-mobile entrance that is $\frac{2}{10}$ mile east of Morehouse Road, or $4\frac{1}{2}$ miles west of the western bridge over the Big Bay of Piseco Lake. The trailhead is marked in winter but can be hard to spot at other times. The trail itself is also marked and is easy to follow as it heads southeast and then east along the route of the old road to Sheriff Lake shown on old topographic maps. Stay on the trail as it heads uphill for little over a mile, until you are well into a valley between two unnamed mountains. The one on the north lies between Route 8 and the trail; Indigo and Jones lakes are cupped high in the one on the south. Now head south on a bushwhack, climbing for a little over $\frac{1}{8}$ mile. Near the top of the hill, you will come to a wide logging road made within the last few years. Follow the road back west (right). It will lead you 1 mile south to the lakes, which are below road level and surrounded by thick woods. The logging road parallels the north shores of both lakes, giving access to the heavily lumbered sections as well as to the woods immediately along the lake, through which you must bush-whack to reach the water's edge.

Indigo Lake has swamps around some of its edges and is a bit smaller than Jones. The latter has a rocky shoreline with some wet and marshy spots but is very attractive. Both lakes are nestled high on the side of the hill, which has summits over 2,400 feet high, both east and west of the lakes. Indigo is 2,200 feet above sea level and Jones about 100 feet higher. The outlet of Jones falls steeply over $\frac{1}{8}$ mile to Indigo.

The eastern end of the logging road you bushwhacked to from the snowmobile trail is difficult to find as it branches off in a con-fusing area of old and new logging roads and snowmobile trails. It is therefore not a good approach to these two mountain lakes or a good connector to Sheriff Lake.

There are two approaches to Sheriff Lake from Route 8. For summer hiking, you should look for the unimproved road shown on the 1954 USGS topographical sheet. Its entrance, which is a bit tricky to locate, begins off an old section of pavement on the south side of Route 8 located just over 2 miles west of the intersection of Route 8 and the West Shore Piseco Lake Road. It begins just uphill and west of a marshy meadow visible from the highway and is concealed by new growth, but it can be identified by two metal posts and a cable that block it to vehicular traffic.

From here, the old road follows a south-southeast course toward Sheriff Lake and is very easy to follow. About two-thirds of the way in, you come upon a lumbered area and clearing where a well-constructed logging road continues toward the lake. When you come to a fork, you will find that the logging road veers right and the old road continues straight ahead and downhill to the water, where a large abandoned and vandalized home, outbuildings, and an overgrown flower garden and fruit orchard line the shores. Most of the lake's shores are wet and marshy.

The second approach is better in winter than summer. Look for a snowmobile trail entrance on the south side of Route 8, a little west of its intersection with the West Shore Piseco Lake Road. It heads southwest and then south to the lake, generally following a road next to the Sheriff Lake outlet. The road is fairly broad and open and is almost suitable for driving in summer, but it makes for dull hiking.

The markings on the snowmobile trail west from Sheriff Lake to the entrance near Morehouse Road and the intersection with the route to Clockmill Corners are scarce. New logging roads in this area further complicate directions, so a through-walk is not recommended.

II

Along
the Adirondack Park's
Southern Boundary

At the southern edge of the Adirondacks, the Blue Line, which delineates the boundary of the Adirondack Park, is scarcely 20 miles from the Mohawk Valley. Patches of private land are mingled with state Forest Preserve lands in the lowlands where fields and timbered tracts are just beginning to return to forest cover. Several areas were reforested with soft woods and conifers, which have now reached maturity. A network of logging roads provides a system of snowmobile trails, and the few that are notable hiking or ski-touring routes are described in sections 22, 23, and 24.

22 South of Stewart Landing
to Glasgow Mills
Trail; hiking, snowshoeing,
cross-country skiing

The majority of snowmobile trails in the southern Adirondacks that follow abandoned roads over recently cut land or old farmsites are interesting to hikers only as exercise. The trail that connects County Route 119 to Route 10 is a marvelous exception and surprisingly pleasant. Summer field flowers abound in the open stretches, deep woods provide shade in other sections, and the vlies, or dying ponds, are full of birds and ducks. And even though the route is a favorite with snowmobilers in winter, cautious cross-country skiers can enjoy the long trek.

The western end of the trail begins, without adequate markings, on the dirt road that heads east off County Route 119, 2¾ miles southeast of the intersection of Route 119 and Stewart Landing Road. County Route 119 connects Emmondsburg and

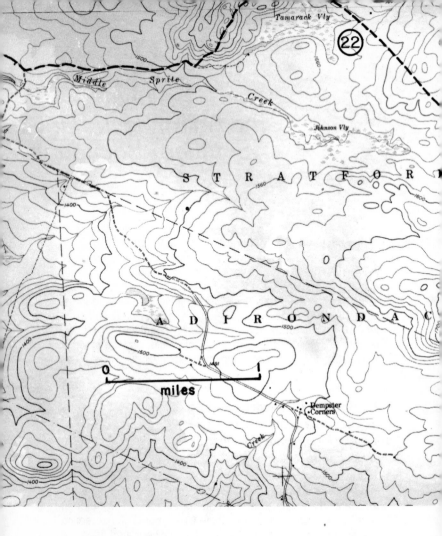

Lassellsville. The dirt road, which the trail follows, begins north of the dammed lake on Middle Sprite Creek. There is a private picnic grounds near the road and the lake.

It is possible to drive more than 1½ miles along the dirt road, farther perhaps in four-wheel-drive vehicles. The best way to enjoy the trail would be to start walking or skiing at this end and have a car waiting at the Route 10 end.

The eastern end of the trail is marked Glasgow Road, which

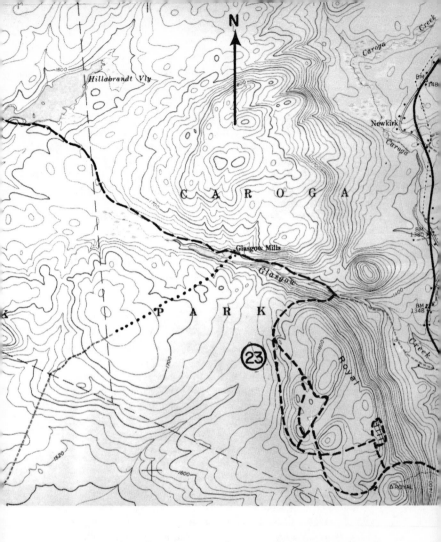

heads west from Route 10, 1¼ miles north of the intersection of Routes 10 and 10A. You will find a small parking turnout 1 mile from Route 10; just beyond it, the road crosses Glasgow Creek on a dilapidated bridge. Do not try to drive across it.

Starting from County Route 119, you will come to a fork in the road in 1¼ miles; the way right leads ¼ mile to a house on a small pond in the large swampy area called Tamarack Vly.

The marked snowmobile route follows the left fork, heading

north for ¾ mile to a little body of water inappropriately called Mud Lake by local people. It is unnamed on the USGS maps. The lake's lovely southern shore has high banks covered with hemlock woods, and you will find several good picnic spots and campsites.

Beyond the lake, the trail turns east, crossing the lake's outlet. The USGS Canada Lake quadrangle shows both this outlet into Tamarack Vly, which drains into Middle Sprite Creek, and an outlet directly west to Sprite Creek. Both exist in high water. The old road traverses land that was once farmed, and the next section is bordered with small trees and many field flowers. In August you will want to stop and pick blackberries.

The trail, still following the old road, swings south of east around Tamarack Vly and 1 mile from Mud Lake passes a cabin near a stream. This marks the end of the dirt road, and the next section, in contrast to the first part of the walk, cuts through deep hardwood forest. Then, as you approach Hillabrandt Vly you will walk through hemlock thickets that appear like a walled corridor carved out of dense woods.

An old dam backs up the water of Hillabrandt Vly, and the trail crosses the outlet on the dam. In the 1930s the vly was a large treeless wet meadow that could be walked in hunting seasons, when it teemed with partridge. Now the dam holds back water nearly to the limits of the vly, with the exception of brushy meadows on the north and northeast. Part of the earthen dam has obviously eroded, but beaver have kept the basic structure intact. After a few dry seasons, the vly could return to meadow, for it is only a shallow body of water filled with pond weeds and water lilies, and hardly more than three feet deep.

Many ducks nest in the swamps below the outlet dam. The vly has several good campsites, all in the hemlock groves that border it.

The trail proceeds east from the dam and then turns southeast toward Glasgow Mills. This section is almost 2 miles long and follows a very muddy dirt road. Unbelievably, the road still bears signs of tire tracks, although it seems impossible that any vehicle could get through, even in dry weather. (They have done so illegally, of course.) The woods gradually change from hemlock to mixed hardwoods to overcut scrubby trees. If you watch carefully you'll notice a parade of different types of roadside plants

Along a snowmobile route in the State Reforestation Area

and ground covers, including a good selection of club mosses.

Glasgow Mills is the site of a manmade lake, fairly shallow now as the dam is much eroded. In the late 1800s, there was a large sawmill and a clothespin factory at Glasgow Mills, but evidence of the small settlement is hard to find. The discerning eye can find the dam, but no sign of the huge wheel that powered the mill. Foundations of several buildings can be traced 100 yards west of the pond and on either side of the road 100 yards east of the pond. Occasional pottery or metal objects protrude from the soil. From Glasgow Mills east to Route 10, a distance of 1¾ miles, the dirt road gradually improves so the last mile can be walked or driven. Heading east, you will cross Glasgow Creek on a worn bridge and then come to the small parking turnout. From here it is just 1 mile to Route 10.

The entire 7½-mile distance to Route 10 can be walked easily in four hours. There are several good picnic and camping spots along the way, and as a nature trail for spring or fall walking, this route is one of the most inviting at the southern edge of the Adirondacks.

A glance at the contours on the USGS map will show you how desirable this is as a cross-country ski route. The long, gentle slopes are perfect. Skiers from Royal Mountain (section 23) often venture this far, as do snowmobilers, so caution is advised. If the through-trip seems impractical, I suggest you start at Glasgow Road and simply ski as far as you like before returning. The succession of forest cover and vistas across the frozen vlies make this trek as varied and interesting in winter as in summer.

An alternative ending to the trail above can be devised using abandoned roads that lead south toward Lassellsville. After crossing the dam at the outlet of the pond by Glasgow Mills, climb the hill to the southwest along a faint but discernible footpath that seems to follow an abandoned road. Within 1 mile the road becomes more obvious and easier to follow. It continues southwest, then more nearly south for 2½ miles more to a left, or east, turn toward the St. Johnsville Reservoir. This point can also be reached by car from Lassellsville.

23 Royal Mountain
Trails; cross-country skiing

A state-marked ski-touring trail connects the road to Glasgow Mills (section 22) with a network of ski trails on top of Royal

Mountain to the south. To take advantage of this network, which was cut partly on private and partly on public lands, follow Glasgow Road west from Route 10 for 1 mile to the small parking area where snowplows turn around. (If the road is not well plowed you might want to park on Route 10 and ski in.)

On skis, head across the bridge over Glasgow Creek; 100 yards beyond the bridge yellow disks appear on your left, marking the route to Royal Mountain. The state trail heads south and then southwest, skirting private land. After climbing Royal Hill it connects with the trail system laid out by local ski-touring clubs and maintained by the Johnstown Ski Team. They gain access to the touring trails on top from the downhill tows of the Royal Mountain Ski Area, but this approach is not generally recommended, because of difficulties on the return. Only experts should attempt

59

to descend the ski area's alpine slopes on cross-country skis, and even then, only the northernmost slope is recommended.

The trail system on top is excellent, designed in rolling terrain through recently logged but still handsome forests. It is roughly a series of loops with spur trails. Coming from the north on the state trail you first encounter the Yellow Loop, which is roughly 2 miles long and may cause difficulties for novices. Bearing left, you will intersect the Green Loop, also nearly 2 miles long; bearing right, you will come to the Apple Tree Loop. Both ends of the Green Loop intersect the Apple Tree Loop on its northern half but east of the Yellow Loop junction.

If you ski counterclockwise around the Apple Tree Loop, the first junction past the Yellow Trail is an unmarked trail that heads directly to Glasgow Mills. At the junction beyond that, an unmarked trail heads west toward the St. Johnsville Reservoir. Then, on the south side of the loop, you come to Big Rock, a huge boulder that could shelter a winter picnic, and the junction with the Big Loop. The Big Loop is 2½ miles long and circles by the head of a Royal Mountain Ski Area tow. A very steep trail branching off its west side connects with Route 10 near Rockwood Lake.

Unfortunately, the descent via the state trail back to Glasgow Road is too steep for novice-intermediate skiers to negotiate, especially the section near Glasgow Creek. The state trail is also poorly marked and maintained, which doesn't help matters.

Current advice and maps are available at the ski area.

24 State Reforestation Area near Rockford
Abandoned roads; cross-country skiing

Skiers from Johnstown and Gloversville have discovered the State Reforestation Area near the intersection or Routes 10, 10A, and 29 by Rockwood. The mature evergreen forests make a beautiful setting for a cross-country ski trip. The roads through the area are unmarked and ungroomed, but parts are suitable for skiers of novice to intermediate ability. The sections south of Route 29 are so clearly defined that no marking is necessary.

The easiest trek is a loop that begins at the intersection of Routes 29 and 10A. On the south side of the intersection, an entrance to the reforestation area is marked with stone pillars, remnants of CCC work in the 1930s. The western entrance of the loop is 9/10 mile west on Route 29, again marked by stone pillars.

The loop itself is 1 ½ miles long, and when snow covers the ever-greens, no handsomer trail can be found. Snowmobiles also use the area, and you might wish to follow their tracks along some of the other abandoned roads. Less than ¼ mile from the start, a road heads east toward an old cemetery. Near the western end of the loop, ⅓ mile from Route 29, a major spur heads southwest toward a hill east of Caroga Creek. This section is steeper than the major loop, but is still suitable for cross-country skiers.

There are also old roads to be explored on the north side of Route 29. There are two entrances to the area, one almost oppo-site the western end of the loop above. But the prettiest and easiest entrance is through the stone pillars on the west side of Route 10A, some 100 yards north of the intersection with Route 29. Unfortunately, the old woods roads in this area are blocked with blowdowns, and unless you are familiar with the area or can follow tracks of other skiers or snowmobiles, you should consider bushwhacking beyond the first ⅔ mile of road.

Again, you will find no more handsome area for skiing, with dark evergreens framing the roadway. You may want to try to improvise a course, using a map and compass. In fact, a maze of old roads crisscrosses the triangular parcel enclosed by the three highways. Some lead toward small Rockwood Lake and the flows east of it. The rolling terrain and the relatively open forest makes it possible to find ski routes even without roads to guide.

Fulton County plans to mark additional trails in this area, so I suggest you contact the county Chamber of Commerce to sup-plement and update information given here. Some grooming is planned and as of this writing, a temporary trailhead has been established on Smith Road, which heads west from Route 10 south of the junction with Route 29A.

III
Canada Lake

My recent research for the book, *Caroga,* a history of the township that contains Canada Lake, has provided a much richer background for the walks in the vicinity of Canada Lake than was available for the first edition of this guidebook.

In 1865 the Wheeler Claflin Company bought 20,000 acres in the town of Caroga, two-thirds of the entire township and almost exactly the portion that is now Forest Preserve land. The company needed the forest in order to harvest hemlock bark for its tannin, necessary to cure cowhides, which were shipped to the area from all over the United States and from South America.

William Claflin owned numerous shoe factories near Boston, Massachusetts. It was easier to ship the cowhides to the forests for curing than to ship hemlock bark or the tanning liquor to the factory sites. Many tanneries sprang up in the wilderness. The tannery at Wheelerville on the inlet of Canada Lake was one of the Adirondacks' largest. It employed as many as 300 men during the two decades after 1865. A small town sprang up around the tannery, which boasted some of the largest leaching and drying sheds in the Adirondacks.

The company also built a huge sawmill at Pine Lake and constructed a plank road to it north from Wheelerville. A plank road connecting Wheelerville with the railroad at Fonda on the Mohawk had already been completed in 1849.

William Claflin saw more profit in the forests than those he expected to derive from the tanning industry. In 1866 he constructed a huge frame hotel, one of the Adirondacks' first resort

Nick Stoner Island in Canada Lake

hotels, in Caroga on the northeast shore of Canada Lake. The Canada Lake House was five stories high with wide porches overlooking the water. While Claflin himself spent scarcely any time at Canada Lake — a very wealthy man, he later became governor of Massachusetts — his vision began Canada Lake's long history as a resort area, which has spread to encompass the shores of several nearby lakes.

A small stone dam was built on the outlet of the lake to float logs to mills closer to Dolgeville and factories to the west. The dam created a 4½-mile-long outlet stream that was navigable. Vacationers were taken along the 7-mile stretch of lake and outlet by a small fleet of steamers, which provided a most elegant wilderness trip.

Two later hotels, the Auskerada, built in 1887 to replace the Canada Lake House, which had burned in 1883, and the Fulton House, which was erected on the south shore in 1888, continued to attract guests to the southern Adirondacks through the first two decades of the twentieth century. Because travel to the lake was by horse and cart, most early visitors came from the surrounding communities. By 1890 visitors from New York City had discovered the resort, and a colony of artists and writers grew around the shores of the lake. Both hotels have since burned, but the area continues as the hub of one of the prettiest resort areas in the southern Adirondacks.

Canada Lake is on several lists as one of the "ten prettiest" lakes in the Adirondacks. Mountains rise steeply from its shores, although, as in the rest of the southern Adirondacks, they reach less than 1,000 feet above the lake, which is itself on a high plateau, 1,500 feet above sea level.

Today cottages line much of the lake's shore, but the scenery is the same as that recorded in 1819 by Henry R. Snyder in the first written description of the lake. "The lake, the mountains, and the woods are sublime . . . .The lake is walled in on both sides with mountains, each mountain crowned with a majestic peak raised above all its surroundings, and each peak so placed as if designed to watch over the lake." An anonymous author writing in 1845 thought the lake was "the most romantic spot I have ever visited. The surface of the ground rising back from the shore is covered with large irregularly shaped rocks from five to forty feet in diameter, lying entirely above ground, and often tumbling together in mountain masses, lodged and wedged in like driftwood."

Only the forests are changed. Mr. Snyder recorded that the "north shore of the lake was covered with a primitive forest, the pines, spruces, and hemlocks all towering above the hard-wood trees . . . All through the forest, from the tops of the mountains sloping to the shore of the lake, these majestic kings of the primeval glades stood in their dignity and grandeur." Today most of the magnificent evergreens are gone.

Tannery and lumbering sites make archeologically interesting destinations. The network of logging roads that were cut to harvest the trees offers some of the loveliest hikes in the Canada Lake area. Many have been reopened as snowmobile trails, and some are so concealed in new forest growth that it is difficult to believe they ever existed. These old roads, and destinations along them, are described in sections 25 through 38.

25 Wheelerville Tannery Site
Short path; walking, canoeing

Parts of the Wheelerville Tannery exist today. A few of the tannery buildings are standing, converted to other uses. The Nick Stoner Inn on Route 10 was once a barn used by the tannery, with oxen kept on the first floor, horses on the second, and hay above. The Caroga Municipal Building and the Nick Stoner Golf Club Shop occupy the tannery store, through which a roadway once passed, allowing carts to be unloaded from either side. Some nearby homes once belonged to tannery workers.

The Nick Stoner Golf Course covers part of the tannery site and obliterates all signs of the original buildings there. However, remains of two of the largest tannery buildings in the Adirondacks, a leaching shed 475 feet long and a drying shed 525 feet long, can be found beside the inlet of Canada Lake. They were built in 1866. Their foundations are in the woods beside the eighteenth hole of the Nick Stoner Golf Course, 2 miles north of Caroga Lake, adjacent to Route 10. Walk along the edge of the woods from the road beside the golf course for about 200 yards, then head north toward the stream. You should be able to locate the foundations easily and identify the flume through which wastes from the tanning process were flushed into the stream. Huge piles of iron straps, which held barrels together and bound bunches of hides, can be found west of the foundations.

An alternate way to reach the site is by canoe from Canada Lake (see section 39 for directions to launch sites). One-quarter-mile east of London Bridge, the bridge over the inlet, new channels have been cut through the flowed lands. The inlet is the middle of the three main streams. It heads south, then east, through the swamps. Pull your canoe out on the south shore at the very beginning of the rapids, where you will find a footpath. The first 200 yards of walking are wet and buggy, but it takes less than five minutes to reach the beginning of the tannery foundations.

26 Picture Rock
Short path, picnic spot;
walking, picnicking

Because picnic places with a view are so rare in this part of the Adirondacks, Picture Rock above Canada Lake is especially desirable, and no place is more accessible, for it is only 100 yards off Route 10. Where Route 10 climbs north behind Canada Lake on the hill locals call Green Mountain (it is unnamed on the USGS map), look for the first parking turnout on the south side. It has, at its eastern end, a rock cut that is well decorated with hideous scrawls and initials.

A path up the rock outcrop on the south starts just a few feet from the road and parking spot, and it is an easy scramble to the smooth rocky site that area people refer to as Picture Rock. From here you can look west past Canada Lake's distinctive island to West Lake. The cliff is so steep that you almost feel suspended above the lake.

27 Cliffs on Green Mountain
Easy bushwhack; picnicking

There are views from the cliffs on the northwestern summit of Green Mountain as well as from Picture Rock (section 26) on its south shoulder. On this side you overlook Green Lake and Kane Mountain, as well as Canada Lake. Below the top of the cliffs a natural overhang creates a small cavelike area that shelters deer in winter. Luminous moss has been found in the cave. Exploring the cave and the cliff tops is a bit adventurous, but it is a very interesting place and one suitable for a picnic.

As there is no path, you must bushwhack to reach the cliffs. From the north side of Route 10, $\frac{2}{5}$ mile east of the bridge over the channel to Green Lake, head into the woods directly up the mountain in a northerly direction. The route follows the ridge line but for easiest walking keep 200 yards east of the crest.

It is a scant ¼ mile and twenty minutes' scramble through occasionally heavy underbrush to the summit. The cave and cliffs are on the ridgeline just below and northwest of the summit.

Watch your footing near the top of the cliffs. There are places where moss-covered roots overhang them. The view is good only in one spot. Walk north past the cliffs to descend about 25 feet to the level of the cave. There is a natural ledge to follow that extends past the cave about 50 feet so you can make a loop below the cliffs and then scramble back to the ridge.

28 Irving Pond from the West

Dirt road, paths; walking, swimming,
canoeing, snowshoeing, cross-country skiing

The short road to Irving Pond is closed to vehicles part of the time and is not adequately maintained for driving. However, it provides a delightful walk, only ¾ mile long, to a pretty, uninhabited lake with good canoeing and several paths along its shores.

To reach the road, drive northwest of Caroga Lake on Route 10 for just 2 miles to the Nick Stoner Golf Course. The road to Irving Pond begins on the north side of the highway opposite the Caroga Municipal Building. Park near the municipal building or drive along the road for ¼ mile, where there is room at the side for one or two cars to park. Do not block the private driveways.

The road, here dirt, climbs a small hill to the pond, following the outlet stream, which drains into Canada Lake, all the way. The shores nearest the road are privately owned, but over 90 percent of the pond's curving shoreline and numerous hidden bays are on state land. One path follows the east side along the route of an abandoned logging road and intersects a snowmobile route; another, which grows fainter every year, edges the west side, following the route of a former logging road to Bellows and Prairie lakes. Walking around the pond to favorite promontories or picnic spots is fine, but the best way to enjoy the pond is with a canoe or inflatable boat. From the water you can see Hogback Mountain looming above the pond on the northeast. All of the shores have heavily wooded slopes, the water is very clear, and the sand bottom makes good swimming.

The pond is a natural one that has been enlarged so that it is nearly 1 mile long. James Irving erected a dam at the outlet in 1855 and operated a sawmill nearby. Next to the mill he built a substantial home, where he and his family lived for nearly two

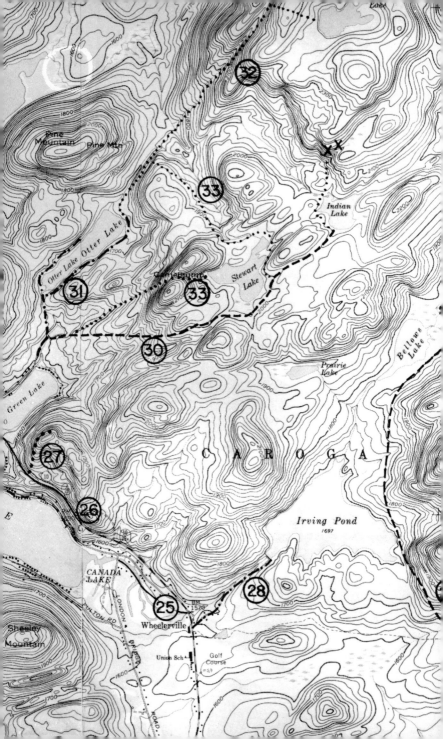

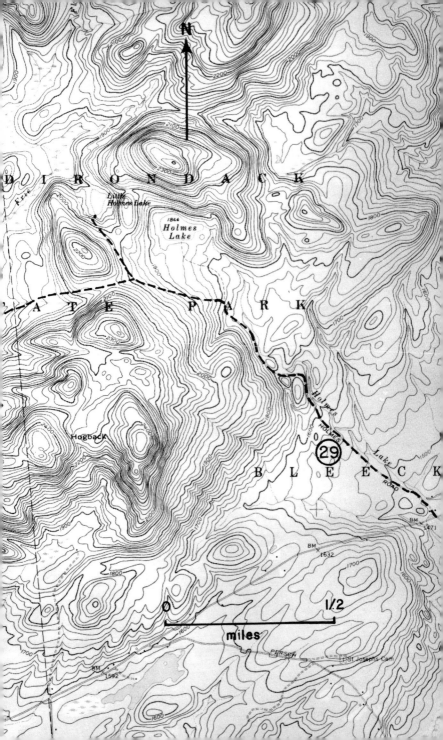

decades. Irving imported the area's first piano so his children might learn to play. The magnificent square instrument survives in a nearby home, but all that is left of the homestead are a few apple trees.

The present high dam was used to regulate water flow into Canada Lake when that lake was used for power. In recent years, the floodgates have been closed, so the lake level has been relatively constant. Now, as soon as you leave the bay by the outlet, the shoreline seems wild and untouched, and only a few twisted stumps in the shallows indicate earlier logging or changes in water level.

In dry times, when there is little flow over the spillway, you can cross the dam to pick up the path on the west shore. In high water, it is safest to hop across on the rocks well below the dam. This path is entirely on state land.

The same route is easier to follow in winter on snowshoes and avoids the snowmobiles that travel near the pond on trails just to the east. Cross the pond and walk along its western edge to the inlet at the north. Keep high and to the west of the stream, traversing a frozen bog and then following the frozen stream to Bellows Lake.

A third path along a roadway on the east shore eventually intersects the snowmobile trail that loops from Benson Road past Bellows Lake (section 29). Beside Irving Pond this path crosses some parcels of private but unposted land. It meets the snowmobile trail at the east end of the pond; the fork is marked. This path is in lovely deep woods, with several views of the pond across the numerous bays.

In winter the dirt road provides an excellent wilderness trek for beginning skiers. The climb to the pond is not too steep, and a loop around its contorted perimeter offers several hours of good skiing. The slight downhill run on the return offers just the right challenge for beginners.

In spring, when the woods are still too wet for walking, the road is a great place to hunt for wildflowers. Beside the outlet and the road you will find a splendid array of spring flowers, among them lady's slippers, may apples, and trilliums.

29 Irving Pond and
Bellows and Holmes Lakes
Trail; hiking, cross-country skiing

East of Caroga Lake a marked and maintained snowmobile trail arcs north from Benson Road through the area just east and north of Irving Pond. Past Bellows Lake and near Holmes Lake, it intersects an old logging road that also runs north from Benson Road. The two routes together describe a nearly 7-mile-long semicircle that makes a delightful hiking or cross-country skiing trek. The area is beautifully varied, with fields, open woods, and dense forests. There is a great range of wildflowers, making this an especially pretty trip in spring and fall.

Walking, the through-trip takes at least four hours, allowing no time for diversions, so it is preferable to hike this route with friends, leaving a car at each end. Then you will have plenty of time for picnicking and two side excursions that can add as much as 3 miles to the trek. Snowshoeing the route is fun, but it is really better on cross-country skis. If you do ski, the trip will be only moderately difficult if you proceed clockwise so that you encounter no difficult downgrades.

The western end of the trail begins along a dirt road that leads north from Benson Road just 2½ miles east of its intersection with Route 10 in Caroga. In summer, it is possible to drive along this road for ⅖ mile. At the end of the dirt road, the trail heads north through the woods, first crossing a wooden bridge over a small stream, and then turns west of north along level ground. After rising along a small hill, still following the bed of an old logging road, it intersects a similar road near the southeast corner of Irving Pond.

At this intersection, 1 $\frac{1}{10}$ miles from Benson Road, the fork left, or west, leads along the south shore of Irving Pond (section 28). The right fork is the snowmobile route you will take toward Bellows and Holmes lakes. It follows an old logging road north through deep woods. After crossing a bridge over a small inlet stream of Irving Pond, it turns east toward Bellows Lake, the entire stretch passing through handsome woods. The distance between the intersection by Irving Pond and the closest approach the trail makes to Bellows Lake is 1½ miles. The trail does not actually lead to the lake; you will have to bushwhack a short distance to see the water. Except for part of the north shore, Bellows Lake is surrounded by marshes. There is a large flow of water from Bellows to Irving, draining also the swamps northeast of Bellows.

Sections of trail in the vicinity of Bellows Lake do not seem to follow any roadbed but rather appear to have been cut expressly for the snowmobile trail. The trail becomes difficult to follow here, and there is a confusing, unmarked intersection near a stream crossing east of the lake. The correct route is the one closer to the lake. Over the next 2 miles the trail is not well marked and has become so overgrown that it could be difficult for inexperienced hikers or skiers to follow.

The eastern end of the 2-mile section again follows the old logging road. Look carefully when the snowmobile trail begins to swing south. Here there is a fork back north to Holmes Lake. It leads ½ mile along an old road to the lake.

South from the intersection the trail along Holmes Road is clear and obvious but unmarked. It is 2 miles from this point out to Benson Road at Peters Corners, 6½ miles east of Route 10. You can drive north on Holmes Road for about 1 mile, and there are a few unposted places where you can pull off, so if you have left your car here you have even less distance left to cover.

Some of the excursions possible off this route are even more interesting than the main trail. The round trip to Holmes Lake from the main trail is only 1 mile. Holmes Lake was named for a family who operated several lumber mills before the turn of the century, one in the vicinity of the lake. It is a very pretty little body of water with a high hill on its north end that seems to dominate the lake. Birding here is very good. The adventurous might wish to circle the lake and climb to the stone ledge on the hill to the north, from which there is a lovely view. There is also a camping spot at the end of the old road, on the south side of the lake.

It is also possible to extend the walk to include a trip to Little Holmes Lake. One-half mile west of the intersection of the Holmes Lake trail and the marked snowmobile trail, still on the latter trail, look for an abandoned roadway heading north. Its beginning is fairly difficult to spot, but it is easy to follow once you're on it. It does not lead directly to Little Holmes Lake, but rather toward a vly to its west called Frie Flow. The logging road used to terminate at the site of a turn-of-the-century logging operation beside the flow. Remnants of the logging camp, stone fireplaces and foundations and a huge rusted boiler that gave steam power to the mill, can still be found on the edge of the flow.

While you are on this old road, look for Little Holmes Lake, a little over ½ mile from the main trail, shortly after the roadway begins to descend. Walking 100 yards to the lake involves a short bushwhack.

30 Stewart and Indian Lakes

Trail; hiking, camping, swimming,
picnicking, snowshoeing, cross-country skiing

The marked snowmobile trail to Stewart and Indian lakes, north-east of Canada Lake, follows an old logging road. This traditional route to the two lakes makes delightful walking. The beginning of the trail is off Green Lake Road, a north turn from Route 10 immediately west of the bridge over the channel between Green and Canada lakes. Drive north for ⅔ mile to the fork where the shore road curves to the right around the north end of Green Lake. The dirt road straight ahead leads to the trailhead. In winter a small area at the intersection is plowed out for trailhead parking. In summer you can drive 200 yards along the dirt road to another parking place.

Walk from either parking area north toward the dam on Fish Hatchery Pond, less than ¼ mile away at the end of the road. The trail used to begin on the dam but now a fancy bridge has been built expressly for snowmobiles across the pond's outlet just below the dam.

The trail immediately passes through a huge garbage dump with shards of broken glass sticking up from the ground. Be careful! However, the rest of the gentle climb toward Stewart Lake, 1¼ miles along the route, is delightful and easy to follow. The official trail is usually dry, except in early spring at the spots where it crosses three intermittent streams. Although most of the surrounding woods were heavily logged some seventy years ago, the forest is composed of mixed hardwoods of good size, providing a handsome cover.

Since the snowmobile trail follows the old road, it does not actually go near Stewart Lake. There are two ways to approach that body of water. You can bushwhack a short way toward the high western shore of the lake as soon as you spot the water glinting through the trees. Nestled below the humps of the Camel-hump, this shore can be explored part way on a footpath. The other approach also involves an easy bushwhack, this one along a barely visible footpath that begins just beyond the swampy southern lobe of the lake. It leads to the eastern shore where one huge rock beckons picnickers and campers.

The snowmobile trail continues another ¾ mile beyond Stewart to Indian Lake, which is shallow but pretty. Little more than an hour is required to hike the 2-mile distance, but that does not allow for a stop at Stewart on the way. You should allow much more time to explore both lake shores, so the trip can easily be extended to a five-hour outing. Either lake is a good, remote camping destination.

If you are adventurous, you might want to try to find the cliffs north of Indian Lake from which there is a view of Stewart Lake, Kane Mountain, the Camelhump, and a small part of Canada Lake. From the outlet of Indian Lake, head due north less than ½ mile on an easy climb through woods that are relatively open after a short span of dense growth near the shore.

There is also a new, unofficial route flagged with red ties from the northernmost point of Stewart Lake northeast through the shallow valley to the west shore of Indian Lake. If you can find that route, you can use it as one of the legs of a loop between the two lakes. To complete the loop, use the snowmobile trail and short bushwhacks along the west shore of Indian and the east shore of Stewart.

You may find that a winter trip on snowshoes is even more fun than a summer hike, for then it is easier to walk around the lake shores. However, if you plan to snowshoe, you will probably want to extend the trek with one of the variations mentioned in section 31. Cross-country skiing the route is a bit of a challenge, but the trail is wide enough for intermediate skiers. Note that if you do ski this trail, you can safely bushwhack to Stewart Lake, but the other variations mentioned here are suitable in winter for snowshoers only.

31 Otter Lake
Path; walking, fishing, picnicking, canoeing, cross-country skiing, snowshoeing

The walk to Otter Lake is hardly more than a stroll but the ½-mile-long lake is beautiful and fun to explore. Trout fishing has been good in the lake at times, and you might want to carry a canoe or an inflatable boat. The two routes described here are both good for snowshoes and not too difficult for skis.

Both routes to Otter Lake start from Fish Hatchery Pond (see section 30 for parking instructions). A private road extends past the pond to a private camp on Otter Lake. The lake is entirely state-owned with the exception of the area around this camp. No vehicles are permitted on the road, but start walking along it, descending to cross the outlet on a small bridge, and then continue on an obvious path beside the stream toward the lake. East

74

of the camp, you should turn northeast along a footpath that continues on the eastern shore of Otter Lake. Be sure to avoid the section of private land around the camp. A good path continues for ½ mile along the lake's east shore, leading to several picnic rocks or fishing spots.

The second route begins exactly west of the Fish Hatchery Pond dam. Its beginning is faint and the barely visible foot tread continues north-northwest into the woods. The path is so overgrown you may not even notice a fork ¼ mile from the beginning. You want to angle right, heading more northerly toward the western shore of the lake. Your first approach is in a swampy area beyond which a lovely hemlock-covered promontory juts into the lake. There used to be a well-worn path around the western shore, but it, too, is now overgrown. However, the forest cover is fairly open, and you can easily follow the shore there.

Lack of use has made the path opposite the dam so difficult to spot that you should take a map and compass and consider this trek a short, easy bushwhack. It is the preferred route to Otter Lake, though, because it clearly avoids all private land.

32 Eastman Lake
Difficult bushwhack; camping, fishing

There is no path to Eastman Lake today, although in the early part of this century there was a logging road to it through the inlet valley of Otter Lake, between Pine Mountain and the Camelhump. This area is now unbelievably rugged and tangled with falls and blowdowns. Old maps name this body of water Oxbarn Lake, some say for the oxbarn that was constructed there for the logging operation. One old-timer disputes this derivation, claiming that the name Oxbarn on the 1890 USGS map predates the logging activity. He says that two surveyors were rechecking their figures in a local bar, desperate for names for the myriad lakes, and pulled that one out of the air. The origin of the more recent name, Eastman, is equally mysterious.

Eastman Lake, a pretty little pond ringed with low hills, is due north of Indian Lake. You can reach it by using the Stewart and Indian lakes snowmobile trail (section 31) to reach Indian Lake, and then bushwhacking. A course of true north from Indian, keeping to the west of the swampy areas, is best, but you should note that this requires keeping a straight course in rugged terrain for a distance of over a mile, not a small feat. The walk to Indian

Lake on the trail takes an hour, the walk around to its north shore over a half-hour, and the bushwhack to Eastman another hour at least.

Friends who use the inlet valley of Otter Lake as a bushwhack route to Eastman Lake consider it equally difficult, both for walking and navigating. This approach is for expert bushwhackers only. To begin the trek, walk north on Otter Lake's eastern shore (section 31) to the inlet, and then bushwhack northeast through the valley along the inlet until it makes a right-angle turn toward Stewart Lake. Leave the stream here and continue northeast to the col in the saddle of the hill just west of Eastman. About halfway along the col's relatively long level, you should head east and over the ridge to Eastman. This trip takes over two and a half hours each way.

When you do finally reach the lake, you might wish to imagine how it looked before the turn of the century, before the forest was logged. Old-timers remember that there was no vegetation below the trees on the east side of the lake, and there was a large blue heron rookery on the shore. After the huge trees were logged, heron were never seen at Eastman Lake again.

33 Stewart and Indian Lakes/Bushwhacks
Easy and moderate bushwhacks; snowshoeing

Three bushwhacks in the vicinity of Stewart and Indian lakes make ideal snowshoe treks. Circling Stewart Lake's swampy shores is much easier in winter than in summer, and from the frozen surface you are better able to appreciate the picturesque lake nestled below the Camelhump with twisted stumps and spires dotting the white landscape.

The easiest walk is the dramatic loop through the humps on the Camelhump. This winter bushwhack first involves snowshoeing up the snowmobile trail to Stewart Lake (section 30), a one-hour trip. This time of year the lake is easily visible from the trail. Cross the frozen surface to the little bay beneath the Camelhump and continue west up a mere 300 yards into the notch between the humps. A little stream flows out of this notch and down into the west end of Stewart Lake; its valley serves to identify the winter route.

The Camelhump

The notch is full of big rocks, and the most interesting walk is beneath the sheer rock wall that forms the north face of the south-west hump. In winter Otter Lake can be seen off to the right. A natural ramp continues to the west, with the face of the south-west hump above to the left and another cliff dropping off to the right. This cliff, which forms the face of the northeast hump, is covered with small spruce trees. In cold weather the rock ledges below the humps have lovely ice formations. Their tops are just rounded off, with no definitive edges and no views, so stay back from them.

Continue west to level land at the bottom of the ramp and then turn southwest, paralleling the face of the mountain. Still pursuing a southwesterly direction, continue for ½ mile until you intersect the snowmobile trail. You are now within twenty minutes' walk of the Fish Hatchery Pond. The ½-mile section contains two inter-mittent streams that are often open in late winter. Even though they are small, use care crossing them. With a picnic in the protected bay, this snowshoe trek usually takes four hours.

A second bushwhack is more difficult and can be made in either winter or summer. Again follow the snowmobile trail to Stewart Lake. Walk around to the west side toward the outlet. In summer the last 200 yards can be very brushy. Follow the outlet for ¼ mile until cliffs begin to form to the south. Turn south to explore the cliffs, which lie along the shoulder of the Camelhump, facing Pine Mountain. They form a long, rugged, and dramatic chain with vertical drops of over 50 feet.

Now walk around the southern end of the cliffs to the valley of the Otter Lake inlet and follow the stream south-southwest to the easy path along the eastern shore of Otter Lake (section 31). The last part of the walk through the valley can be difficult. The entire walk, from the Fish Hatchery Pond trailhead around Stewart Lake to the cliffs, then to Otter Lake and out to the parking place on the extension of Green Lake Road, requires a minimum of four hours.

A third walk — also a winter bushwhack — starts along the snowmobile trail, cuts back southwest to the outlet of Stewart Lake, runs along the outlet toward Otter Lake, and finally edges along Otter Lake back to the start of the snowmobile trail. Remember that the 1¾-mile walk along the Stewart Lake outlet can be tricky at two points, both in swampy areas where care must be taken to find the stream bed on the opposite side. The outlets of Indian and Stewart lakes flow remarkably close together, then part, going in totally different directions. Several hikers have been confused by their proximity. Stewart Lake's outlet flows west, then northwest, and finally southwest past several beautiful little pools, with delightful falls and rock formations. The 6-mile total circuit, which takes four and a half hours in winter, is strenuous both in summer and in winter and requires the use of map and compass.

34 Kane Mountain
Trails, paths, bushwhack; hiking

Kane Mountain provides a variety of adventures, the traditional one being a climb to the fire tower, which is manned from May through October. The observer's days off are Monday and Tuesday, so don't plan on hiking the mountain those days. On moderately clear days you can enjoy the views of Pine Lake to the north and the long outlet of Canada Lake to the west. On really clear days the view unfolds to include the mountains of the Silver Lake Wilderness interior, with Hamilton Mountain visible in the northeast. The view north along the mountains that rim the Sacandaga River Valley ends with the hills behind Piseco Lake and T Lake Mountain.

The most spectacular vista is across the Mohawk Valley, southeast to the Helderbergs and south to the Catskills, where Blackhead, Black Dome, and Thomas Cole stand out as a cluster of giant rounded peaks. There is no view from the wooded summit itself, so it is fortunate that the tower is still open.

The most traveled route is a ½-mile-long steep climb from the south on a marked trail. It begins on Schoolhouse Road, which is a right, or north, turn off Route 10, ¼ mile west of the bridge between Canada and Green lakes. You will find the trailhead and room to park about 100 yards from Route 10.

Even though the trail rises nearly 600 feet from the road to the tower, the rock-strewn route can be conquered in twenty minutes. The trail is well used, and you should have no trouble following the foot tread, although in places walking is difficult because of exposed roots and loose rock.

Two other approaches are informal paths, either of which can be combined with the trail to make a circuit of the mountain. For the path on the east, drive or walk along Green Lake Road to the parking turnout on the route to Fish Hatchery Pond (section 30). If you park at the Schoolhouse Road trailhead and walk the complete circuit, note that the road distance from there to the beginning of this path is under 1 mile, about twenty minutes' walking time.

Beginning opposite the parking turnout, the path follows a road that was cut up the mountain to haul materials for the ranger's cabin. The path is considerably less steep than the heavily traveled trail on the south and is a good alternate route. No attempt has been made to keep the roadway clear, so blowdowns and new growth occasionally obscure the trail, which passes through an area of huge and beautiful hardwoods. Look carefully if you are walking in midsummer, for you will be certain to find rattlesnake orchids along the first quarter of the way. The path emerges in a ferny meadow north of the tower. Forty minutes will suffice to cover the ¾-mile distance.

The second path is informally identified in places with yellow markers. The path approaches the summit from the north along the steep western ridge of Kane Mountain. It is obviously well traveled and begins in the camping area constructed to the east of the Pine Lake outlet and dam. To reach it, drive north on Route 10 for 1⁶/₁₀ miles past Kane Mountain to the Pine Lake campground. The road through the campground crosses the outlet below the dam. Take a right fork to camp site number 75. The path begins here, although there seems to have been some attempt to conceal the start.

The path heads east, gently climbing for about ¼ mile before swinging to the south to climb rather steeply toward the ridge. The last segment generally follows the long axis ridge of the mountain to the tower. The route is through beautifully wooded country, and deer are often seen here in summer.

The path swings far to the east before ascending the mountain to the south to avoid the steep cliffs on the northwest slopes. It is possible to leave the lower part of the path and bushwhack south to these cliffs, leaving the path less than ½ mile from the start and about two-thirds the way up the steepest part of the climb. Parts of the cliffs are a series of steps, so it is possible to climb their faces. From several places along the top of the ridge there are views to the north over Pine Lake and to the west and southwest. Because the cliffs are well over 100 feet high in places, care should be taken in their vicinity.

The fourth adventure on Kane Mountain is a bushwhack along its northern slopes. A road used to circle the northeast side of Kane Mountain, connecting Pine Lake, Green Lake, and the inlet end of Canada Lake near London Bridge. That road existed before 1840 and was essentially abandoned about 1850 when

Canada Lake's inlet was bridged and the road along Canada Lake's north shore was first constructed. There is no trace of the eastern end of this road, but the western part was used in the early 1900s as a logging road. Even so, this end is so concealed that the trek along it must be considered a bushwhack. It is a beautiful, little traveled route 1⅛ miles long. Because it is a bushwhack, it will take over an hour to hike. If you are adept at following old roads, this route, combined with two informal paths to the summit of Kane Mountain, would provide a full day's circuit.

To find the eastern end of the path, use the Otter Lake path opposite the Fish Hatchery Pond dam (section 31). After a ten-minute walk, about ¼ mile from Green Lake Road, look for a faint left fork. If you notice a long straight stretch filled with small trees, you have found the route. The roadway contoured around the north of Kane Mountain in a long, gentle arc, climbing less than 160 feet from the level of the Fish Hatchery Pond. Of course, you will have a map and compass.

The western end intersects the path from the Pine Lake campground. Again, there is a faint fork in the path, unmarked. It is ¼ mile east of Pine Lake, less than fifteen minutes' walk along that path.

35 West Caroga Lake toward Stewart Landing

Trail; hiking, cross-country skiing

Immediately after 1810, settlers could purchase 1,000-acre homesteads in the Glen, Bleecker, and Lansing Patent for 18¢ an acre. Homesteaders moved from the east along Benson Road to Five Points, the area around an intersection on Route 10 just north of the present community of Caroga Lake. A road from the Five Points extended west into the wilderness south of the Canada Lake outlet. That road today is marked as a snowmobile trail.

The first stretch, to a natural grassy meadow that was the site of one of the area's first farms, is today a lovely 2¾-mile trek. The farm site was abandoned before 1850. It takes an hour and a half to reach the meadow, where old pumps and pipes, iron wheels, and other remains of the farm can be found.

If you are using the New York State DEC "Snowmobile Guide" for directions here, please note that it does not show the trail correctly. The DEC map is based on the 1901 edition of the USGS map for this area, on which the outlet of Mud Lake is improperly drawn. The route is no longer the mystery trek this error caused the first time I explored the trail. Superimposing old maps that indicate the road onto the most current USGS survey map gives a fairly accurate picture of the route the road actually takes.

The round-trip walk begins at the end of Morey Road, the westernmost of the Five Points, a left turn off Route 10, just ¼ mile north of Caroga Lake. Park at the end of Morey Road. The trail starts as a continuation of the road. The walk is pleasant and easy, on a relatively level grade through open forests with mature trees and a beautiful woods floor of ferns and Solomon's seal and sessile merrybells. The route is generally west; then, in the ½ mile before the meadow, it swings northwest, descends a small hill, and crosses a tiny stream, where the meadow comes into view to the west. The trail swings around to the north and into the meadow.

The trail heads west from the outlet that drains the meadow, with easy walking for less than ½ mile. It then continues 3 miles west to a point south of Stewart Landing, skirting large swampy areas that are not good for hiking. The western end of the trail is also full of brambles, so warm-weather hikers are advised to use only the first part described.

In winter the trail is heavily used by snowmobiles, but it is otherwise delightful as a cross-country ski route, especially after a light snowfall frosts the machine-packed course. Then your trip west beyond the meadow is limited only by the distance you can travel.

36 Pine Lake
Path along old road; walking, canoeing

Once you get past the amusement park at the south end of Pine Lake, just off Route 10 to the north of Canada Lake, you discover this beautiful mountain lake. Pine Lake can be explored peacefully by canoe or from the fine path that edges its western shore.

To reach both the canoe launch site and the start of the footpath, turn east off Route 10 by the signs for the amusement park, drive through the park, and then turn left onto the road that follows Pine Lake's west shore for ½ mile. Park at the road's end.

Launch your canoe and paddle north; it's possible to continue in this direction for 1 mile, until you reach a swamp dotted with the stumps of trees killed when the level of the lake was artificially raised by the dam at the southern (outlet) end. Linear patterns of the upturned stumps' roots are beautifully silhouetted against the quiet water of the lake's upper end, which seems to disappear into the swamp. You will be surprised and delighted by this area's apparent remoteness, and if you enjoy photographing nature, you can certainly spend several hours exploring the stump gardens and water plants.

The footpath also runs for 1 mile from the parking area toward Pine Lake's northern end. Following a well-constructed old logging road that was in places raised above swampy areas on a base of large stones makes a pleasant hour's walk. The wild-flowers of the deep woods, ferns, and saprophytes enhance the short woods walk, and there are lovely views east across the lake.

This path also gives access to the two low hills just to the west that are lined with huge boulders and short cliffs. No walk along the lakeshore would be complete without exploring some of these, and in fall the view from the tops of some of the knolls is especially nice. Surrounded by lovely hills, Pine Lake is dominated by Kane Mountain on the south, Pine Mountain on the east, and a small hill area people call "Roundtop" to the northeast; all cast magnificent reflections on the quiet waters of the lake's northern end.

Two streams drain into the lake, both passing through swampy valleys. The easternmost valley is inaccessible, but it is possible to cross the one from the north to a small plateau covered with huge hemlocks and large open areas beneath the trees. A narrow path used by hunters continues along the swamp, on the other side of the stream north-northeast onto a shoulder of Roundtop before it completely disappears.

37 Negro Lake
Easy bushwhack

One of the many fascinating bogs in the region is Negro Lake, named for the brown color of its water. The varieties of plants that have adapted to life in this quaking bog and its sterile, acid environment are fascinating. You might even enjoy, as I do, mucking about here in the ooze, searching out the lovely wildflowers (for a more accessible bog, see Chub Lake, section 61).

When the water of Canada Lake is very high, it is possible to navigate the stream from Negro Lake Bay, at the southwest end of Canada Lake, for nearly ½ mile south. When you can paddle no farther use this outlet as a guide, and walk south along it for

Stumps in Pine Lake

¼ mile, where it splits. To reach Negro Lake, follow the stream to the left, east, for just over ¼ mile. (The other stream drains Mud Lake and a nearly dry beaver meadow.)

On the bushwhack to Negro Lake you will pass a couple of lovely small falls. The lake itself is surrounded with fields of grass, which give way to floating masses of sphagnum moss.

There are other bushwhack routes to the lake, mostly used by hunters, but all of the surrounding terrain is rugged and difficult. These other routes are best for winter travel when the swampy shores of several small ponds and vlies do not impede travel (see section 38).

38 West Caroga Lake to
Canada Lake via Negro Lake
Winter bushwhack; snowshoeing

The route from West Caroga Lake to Canada Lake via Negro Lake is recommended only for winter use because it passes through swampy terrain. These swamps, frozen and accessible in winter, are the most attractive features of the winter trip.

I suggest you leave one car at each end and make it a one-way trek. On the south, or starting end, follow the town road along the north shore of West Caroga Lake to its end, where in winter there is room to park one or two cars. You finish this trek at the small parking turnout at the end of the road along the south shore of Canada Lake. Both roads are plowed.

From the end of the road at West Caroga Lake, snowshoe down to the frozen stream bed which will provide the course for the first quarter of the route. The stream flows from a small draw. You intersect the Caroga Lake-Stewart Landing snowmobile trail (section 35) ½ mile west, up the draw. Continue across the trail through the end of the draw in a west-northwest direction for ¼ mile to Mud Lake. Cross Mud Lake to its outlet and then follow that stream west and north for ¼ mile. When it bends west, you can either continue toward magnetic north, cross-country to Negro Lake, or follow the outlet through another vly, using the frozen stream to lead you to the Negro Lake outlet, which you then walk up to reach the lake.

From Negro Lake head north to climb the shoulder of a hill. Follow the ridgeline angling slightly east to a cliff where there's a fine view of Negro Lake. There is also a view east-northeast along the steep northern face of Sheeley Mountain.

Continue on high ground, winding generally northeast, over the hill to bluffs with views of Canada and West lakes. Descend the long ridge northeast directly to the parking area at the end of the south shore road. The 3½-mile trek usually takes about three hours.

IV
Canada Lake Outlet and Sprite Creek

The nineteenth-century dam at Stewart Landing on Sprite Creek was designed to serve the lumber mill on the outlet of Canada Lake, but the long, navigable channel it created provided a great adventure for vacationers staying at the hotels on the eastern end of the lake. Imagine a day-long excursion on a thirty-foot steamer with ladies wearing hoop skirts and wide-brimmed hats to protect them from the sun and the smoke that belched from the steamer's smokestacks. Often the steamers would pull a chain of rowboats full of extra passengers.

Today's adventures along the outlet and Sprite Creek are not as elegant perhaps, but there are several trips that certainly can be as much fun.

The outlet of Canada Lake, Sprite Creek, flows west to join the East Canada Creek, which courses south to the Mohawk River. The drainage patterns in the vicinity of the lake are curious because you have no sense of a height-of-land in the area. Just south of Canada Lake, the Caroga Lakes flow south toward the Mohawk, entering that river a dozen miles east of the East Canada Creek's confluence. But just north of the Stoner Lakes, which are the northernmost sources of Canada Lake, water flows into the West Branch of the Sacandaga. That river makes a circuitous route north, then east, to empty into the Hudson at Luzerne, over 50 miles "as the crow flies" from where Canada Lake's waters enter the Mohawk.

39 Canada Lake Outlet
Canoe trip

Four hours of paddling are required for the round trip from Canada Lake, through Lily Lake, to the dam at Stewart Landing and back. It is strenuous exercise, but it makes a handsome canoe outing, especially in spring or fall when few motorboats are in the water yet. The presence of motorboats and the recent construction of cottages along the western shores of the outlet stream keep this area from being called wilderness, but sections still appear remote and lovely.

There are two public boat-launching sites on Canada Lake, one at a fishing access on West Lake Road, and the other, for which there is a small fee, in the vicinity of the store at Canada

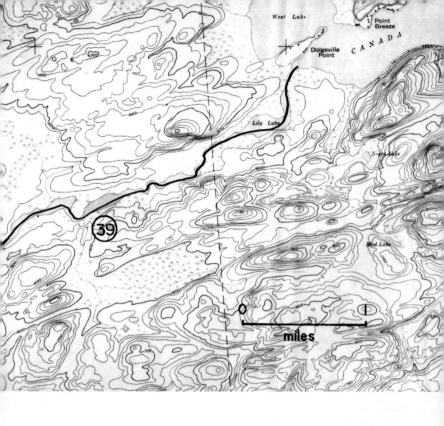

Lake, on the northwest side of Route 10, less than ¼ mile from the bridge over the channel between Canada and Green lakes. To reach the fishing access, take the left, or south, turn from Route 10, 1 mile northwest of the bridge between Canada and Green lakes. The road is marked with signs for the fishing access. Take the right fork 100 yards from Route 10, and park on the west side of "Sawdust Creek," the outlet of Pine Lake that provides a short channel to West Lake.

From West Lake, canoe south to Canada Lake, then west into Lily Lake, which is surrounded by state land. There is a campsite on the south side of Lily Lake, below the hill. Most of the Lily Lake shore is heavily wooded, low, and wet, so there are only a few places on state land where you will find a spot near the water that is high and dry enough for camping. Lily Lake has the requisite lily pads and a good variety of other water plants. Wood ducks and mergansers are often found in the pickerelweed, and if you are fortunate you may spot a pair of loons.

West of Lily Lake, the channel narrows, twisting and turning through rock-lined shores. The stream is smooth and easy, with little current in summer, and the few rocks in the channel are not apt to bother canoes. Look for the rocks at the western end of Lily Lake and in the large narrow horseshoe bend 2 miles beyond Lily Lake. The channel is so narrow in several places that it is difficult to imagine how loaded steamers made it the entire way to the dam at Stewart Landing.

The water in Canada Lake is regulated by the dam and is usually lowered a foot in early fall, and more by the end of November. Repairs to the dam have necessitated changes in recent years, so check the level if you are planning an off-season canoe trip. There is a gauge at the bridge between Canada Lake and Green Lake that measures water level in feet above sea level. Summer level is just under 1,543 feet. Below 1,541 feet, a canoe trip becomes difficult; below 1,539 feet it is impossible.

From the launching site behind the store at the eastern end of Canada Lake to its outlet into Lily Lake, the distance is 2½ miles, and from there to the Stewart Landing dam is almost 4½ miles. The distance from the fishing access through West Lake to the entrance to Lily Lake is almost 1½ miles.

40 Along Sprite Creek
Picnic spots, short path;
picnicking, walking

The nineteenth-century mill dam across the outlet of Canada Lake at Stewart Landing was superceded in 1912 by a higher dam built ¼ mile downstream. This one channeled water through a long wooden flume to a generating station downstream on Sprite Creek. The ten-foot-diameter flume with its huge metal rings has disappeared, but the remnant of a surge tower, which controlled the rush of water from the lake, still stands west of Stewart Landing near Sprite Creek.

An abandoned roadway leads past the surge tower, now only a huge cement scaffold looming incongruously in the woods. You

Canada Lake Outlet

can use the roadway as a route to the tower or to the nearby creek. It's a good route for a short walk and provides access to a handsome section of stream with a series of little waterfalls and rapids.

Drive east from Stratford ¼ mile on Route 29A, and then go south 2⅓ miles on the road to Emmondsburg. At Emmondsburg, head east on County Route 119 for approximately 3 miles, where you bear right, or south, on Middle Sprite Road. That road makes a loop with the county road. Drive south on Middle Sprite Road less than ½ mile to the height-of-land where the road turns east. Here a smaller dirt road forks right, or south.

Park and walk south for less than ¼ mile, until the road forks again. Turn left, or east, to see the surge tower.

If you continue straight, or southeast, you will notice that the land on the west is posted. This road leads to Sprite Creek, where the land to the east is not posted. Walk upstream to enjoy several waterfalls and picnic sites.

On your outing to the picnic spot beside the surge tower, you might also want to visit Stewart Landing. Stewart Landing Road is a north turn from County Route 119, less than ½ mile west of the western end of the Middle Sprite Road loop. The 8½-mile-long dirt road takes you right to the dam.

V

Between Stratford and Pine Lake

A dozen long, flat routes have trailheads on Route 29A between Stratford on the west and Pine Lake on the east. Around these old logging roads much of the forest cover is small and scrubby, and some of the trails are muddy and wet. However, a few do reach interesting distant lakes.

Most of the trails are designated for snowmobile use, but their use by these machines has been declining. Furthermore, area snowmobile groups are remarkably tolerant of other users, so these trails have become favorites in recent years for snowshoers and cross-country skiers. They are ideal for all winter sports.

41 Nine Corner Lake

Trail; hiking, cross-country skiing, snowshoeing, fishing, camping, swimming

The snowmobile trail to Nine Corner Lake is about 1 mile long, very easy to walk or ski, and all too accessible. While the lake is one of the prettiest in the region, it has become so popular there seem to be campers there throughout the summer, and even small crowds on weekends. But the offerings here are incredibly diverse, from earliest spring when the trail sides are good places to find wildflowers, to summer when the swimming is good, through fall when the woods blaze with color, and into winter when the long flat route beckons beginning snowshoers and cross-country skiers.

Snow cover helps obliterate the recent destruction of shoreline vegetation and the several garbage caches that keep accumu-

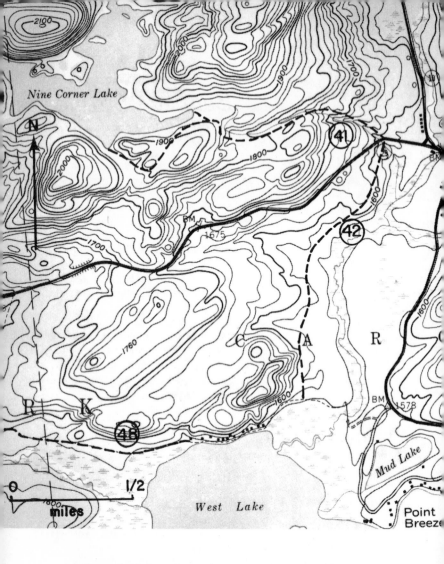

lating. In the mid-1970s, Nine Corner Lake was limed to counteract the acid rain and then stocked, so that trout fishing here in the spring of 1978 surpassed that of many surrounding lakes. The effects of this heavy fishing and camping use are already all too obvious. In spite of the lake's great beauty, if you are seeking a pristine lake you would be advised to limit your visits to winter.

This is one lake where a boat is very desirable, and the width and grade of the trail make it possible to carry a canoe to it with relative ease. From the water, the lake has many hidden and unusual spots, deep bays that are hard to reach by land, and small islands. Almost every time I have visited Nine Corner Lake, I have seen loons diving and reappearing in its northern reaches. The water is cool and exceptionally clear, so it is doubly unfortunate that many careless campers have so dirtied the campsites and trail.

The designated snowmobile trail, which traces an old roadway, begins on the north side of Route 29A, just 300 yards west of the intersection of Route 10 at Pine Lake. The trail crosses the lake's outlet stream in about ½ mile, in an area of lovely little falls, and reaches a short cutoff path to the outlet in another ½ mile.

The outlet end of the lake has sharp rock bluffs from which people like to swim and a campsite that is high and dry. Very few of the lake's many corners are visible from here, but a short path to the north offers wider views. This path across the remains of the dam at the outlet used to disappear after a few bends. It is amazing how far it has been extended in the last few years, just because there are so many more people walking around toward the north end of the lake.

The snowmobile trail continues along the lake's south shore, leading to several picnic spots on rock outcrops high above the water. It generally follows the route of the first road from Pine Lake west. The extension west beyond the lake holds little interest for hikers.

Winter travelers to Nine Corner Lake can ski or snowshoe across the frozen lake to the northern lobe with its several small spruce- and hemlock-covered islands, which provide shelter for a winter picnic. Please note on your return that the last 300 yards before Route 29A are steep and will provide a considerable challenge to novice skiers.

42 West Lake
Trail; hiking, cross-country skiing

A new route has been cut expressly for snowmobiles to connect the road to West Lake with the trail to Nine Corner Lake. For a short walk in spring and summer, the trail is surprisingly interesting. In winter, it makes a fun ski route.

The northern end of the trail is directly opposite the trail to Nine Corner Lake (section 41). Look for it on the south side of Route

29A, just 300 yards west of Route 10. The southern end of the trail is on the road from Route 10 to West Lake, about halfway between the lake and the boat-launching site described in section 39.

The trail heads south from Route 29A, crosses the outlet of Nine Corner Lake, skirts the outlet of Pine Lake (which is also the inlet to West Lake) and the flows beside it, then continues in deep, rich woods for 1⅜ miles to the West Lake road. The route is a fine nature trail (pileated woodpeckers are often seen near its northern end), and the terrain is so gentle that walkers of all ages can enjoy it. A one-way walk requires no more than forty-five minutes.

Skiers should note that there are three fancy snowmobile bridges on this stretch, which they should approach carefully, for the short slopes beside them can seem unexpectedly steep.

43 Fourth Lake, Third Lake and Long Lake
Trail; hiking, cross-country skiing, snowshoeing, camping, fishing, picnicking

It is discouraging to hikers that parts of the new marked snowmobile trails, which admittedly follow old logging roads, often traverse flat swampy areas whose frozen surfaces turn to impenetrable quagmires in summer. This is true of sections on the trail to Fourth, Third, and Long lakes, which cannot be walked in summer except in a severe drought. However, all these trails have been discovered by other winter travelers, so that use by showshoers and cross-country skiers has been increasing.

This snowmobile trail describes a loop with both ends on Route 29A. The eastern trailhead is freshly marked and has been given a new trailhead parking turnout. The turnout is on the south side of NY 29A, 3 miles west of Pine Lake and ¾ mile east of Pleasant Lake. The trailhead is opposite, on the north side of the highway. Signs at the trailhead give the distance to Spectacle Lake (6 miles) and Dexter Lake (6.5 miles), but they do not acknowledge the fact that the trail first passes Fourth and Third lakes.

The western end of the trail is the continuation of a dirt road that branches off the road along the east shore of Lake Pleasant, about ½ mile north of Route 29A. This section traverses private but unposted lands, which bear the traditional state notice that permission to cross may be required.

The eastern half of the loop is the most interesting, but it contains the sections that can be too wet in summer. As a result, the western half is the route recommended for summer when a loop is not always possible. In winter, of course, the trail is passable from end to end.

Starting on the east, the trail follows an abandoned logging road, to which new snowmobile bridges have been added. The fact that it can be so wet is hard to understand in light of its earlier use as a logging road. The trail heads generally north over flat, boggy ground, passing through logged areas of both hard and soft woods. At first, the trail skirts the east side of a wet meadow adjacent to the Burnt Vly stream. There's a drier, wooded stretch, and then, after about 1 mile, a long chain of flowed lands, Burnt Vly. It continues for another 1 ½ miles east of these swamps. At 2½ miles the trail swings a little west and crosses the Burnt Vly stream. You will have climbed less than 140 feet in elevation from the start. The trail swings east of north 1 mile farther on and ¼ mile later crosses the outlet of Goose Egg Lake.

At this point you are west of Fourth Lake. The trail heads toward an abandoned settlement that used to lie between Third and Fourth lakes. Beaver have recently flooded the area between the two lakes, obliterating all traces of the settlement and most of the trail. In the past, it was possible to bushwhack south toward Fourth Lake from the grassy opening near the junction of the trail and the outlet. Beaver have made this a wet and impossible job, but conditions are bound to change again.

It appears that the new snowmobile trail does not exactly follow the old logging road in this area, perhaps in an effort to thwart the beaver. Water level permitting, you may want to poke around for the former settlement. I've discovered a huge pile of old tin cans and a few pitchers and pieces of pottery, but no foundations for the buildings. This was a logging camp, and it appears to have been used in the early part of this century.

The trail continues north, skirting Third Lake on its west also. Near the northwest corner of the lake there is a campsite often used by fishermen. The logging road continues north toward Spectacle Lake (section 44) and either of two left forks, only one of which is marked, will keep you on the marked snowmobile trail as it loops to Long Lake and then turns south toward Lake Pleasant and Route 29A.

Since summer hikers will most probably approach Long Lake from the south, rather than by Fourth and Third lakes, I'll describe the western half of the loop from its beginning on Route 29A. When the trail leaves the dirt road beside Lake Pleasant, it con-

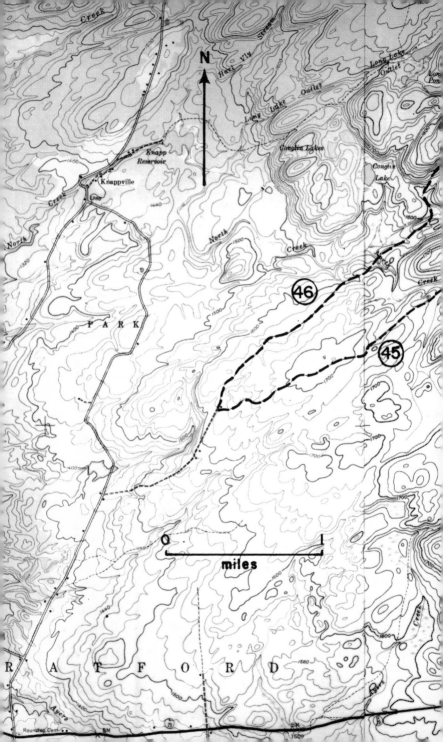

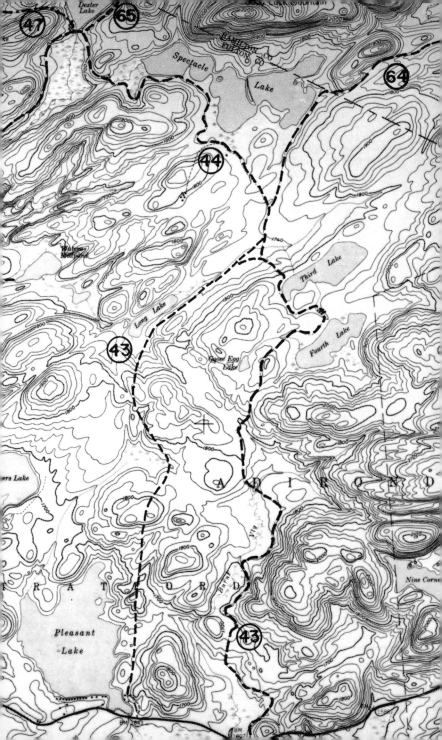

tinues for nearly 2½ miles on a logging road that is still used by cars and four-wheel-drive vehicles. It is certainly not an exciting trail, for much of it is very flat and so recently cut that the timber cover is very small.

You forget how dull the road is when you finally reach Long Lake, though. It is a beautiful little body of water with flat shores that sport several dry rocky spots for picnics.

The trail swings northeast past Long Lake, again through often muddy sections. Just before it crosses the inlet stream, you'll see a path to the right, or east, which constitutes a shortcut to the main snowmobile trail north of Third Lake. If you miss this junction, no matter, for there is a second intersection less than ¼ mile farther on. Here the left fork north heads to Spectacle Lake (section 44) and the right fork heads south to Third Lake and the eastern half of the loop just described.

Fourth, Third, and Long lakes are all long and narrow with their major axes running southwest to northeast. The area surrounding them is flat, and their shorelines are low. Fishing is dominated by warm-water species.

The summer trip to Long Lake is a total of 5 miles, requiring no more than two and a half hours because of the flat terrain. It is a good 8-mile walk to cover the entire loop, one-way. Allow one hour to walk from Long Lake east to Third and Fourth lakes. Since these lakes are also accessible by trails from the east, Route 10, via Spectacle Lake, and from the west via Waters Millpond and Dexter Lake, there are several opportunities here for long one-way walks (see sections 45, 53, and 64). All the routes are easier to follow in winter, after snowmobiles have packed the trails.

44 Spectacle Lake
from the South

Trail; hiking, cross-country skiing,
fishing, snowshoeing, camping

The snowmobile trail past Fourth and Third lakes (section 43) extends north through very flat, wet ground to Spectacle Lake. The dismal part about this trail is that fishermen have used it to drive tractors carrying camping equipment in to Spectacle Lake, illegally, of course. The distance from Route 29A to Spectacle Lake is stated as 6 miles; it may be that far to an area where the ground is not too swampy to camp. Other trails to Spectacle are preferable for hiking, but this route is useful to combine with them (sections 46 and 64).

The snowmobile trail, following the old road north of Third Lake, heads west of north over flat terrain, approaching the southern swampy shore of Spectacle Lake. A left fork near the swamps used to lead to a logging camp. That fork is not obvious. The trail splits again at a second fork. The way left leads to a logging camp ¼ mile west of the outlet of Spectacle Lake, beyond the swamp that surrounds it. The way right leads around swamps on the southeast side of Spectacle Lake and intersects the trail from section 64. The latter stretch is only recommended for winter travel.

45 Waters Millpond
Trail; cross-country skiing, snowshoeing, hiking

Two snowmobile trails lead toward Waters Millpond and intersect ¼ mile to its west. One begins at Seeley Road, which heads north from Route 29A exactly 1 mile east of Stratford. The other, which also heads north from Route 29A, is an extension of a town road 1¼ miles east of Seeley Road. The latter has little interest for hikers. Cross-country skiers might find it useful in creating a loop connecting with the Seeley Road approach, but this requires two cars. For these reasons, I do not describe it in this guide. It is mentioned only so that you will be aware of its existence when you intersect it near Waters Millpond.

The Seeley Road approach to Waters Millpond is the more interesting by far. Because it also provides access to a trail to Dexter Lake (section 46), it offers a much better loop route, both for hikers and for skiers.

Seeley Road is plowed in winter, and its southern half is paved. Near the northern end of the paved section, 1¾ miles from Route 29A, a dirt road branches to the east, extending through private lands for 1 mile before ending. It is possible to drive this section in summer; winter hikers should note that this extra mile must be added to distances mentioned for trips described in this and the following section.

At the end of the dirt road, two rudimentary roads lead into the woods, one on either side of a dilapidated log house. Both roads are now marked snowmobile trails. The road on the right is the one that leads to Waters Millpond. For the first ¾ mile it traverses private land. The route is flat and in recently logged country. It is often muddy. Because it is well marked and open, you need no special directions to follow it. One-quarter mile before you reach the pond's outlet, the trail splits; the right fork is the alternate snowmobile approach from Route 29A. You go left.

Waters Millpond is almost 2½ miles from the log cabin, about an hour's walk in summer. Cross-country skiers should add a half-hour to cover the unplowed stretch of dirt road from Seeley Road. The gentle grade — there is only a change in elevation of about 100 feet — makes this a fairly easy ski route, especially if snow-mobiles have already broken trail.

Much of the area around the pond is swampy. The pond, though a natural one, was enlarged some time prior to the 1901 USGS survey by a flood dam built for logging operations at its outlet. This dam no longer holds, so the pond's entire northwestern section, which must have been only a shallow flooded area then, is now just a large swamp. The wetness makes it difficult to explore the perimeter in summer, but winter travelers can enjoy the stumps poking through the frozen surface.

You will notice that a trail heads northwest from a spot almost at the pond's outlet. This ¾-mile-long section has been cut and marked to intersect the old road to Dexter Lake (section 46), which begins to the left of the log cabin. This short connector starts and ends in a marsh, making it, like the trail to Waters Mill-pond, more attractive for winter traveling.

46 Dexter Lake
Trail; hiking, snowshoeing,
cross-country skiing

The old road to the left of the log cabin described in section 45 leads in 3½ miles to Dexter Lake. The route is so level and the walk so easy that it takes less than two hours to reach the lake's outlet. The trip is one of the more interesting in the area, partly because it can be combined with a walk to Waters Millpond or Knapps Long Lake (sections 45 or 47) and Dry Lake (section 65), and partly because there are several things to see on the way.

The trail heads generally northeast, following an old but wide road bed. Because the route is so well marked, you will need few

Canada lily

special directions to follow it. For the first ½ mile, the road passes through private land. The woods from the log cabin as far as the snowmobile bridge over North Creek, 1½ miles in, have been recently logged. North of the bridge you will skirt a swamp where you might see deer. Next you will pass a pretty little rock-lined ravine. One-half mile farther north, the trail traverses a grassy meadow that appears to have grown up in what may have been a manmade pond. The trail crosses one of the streams flowing through the meadow, using the ruins of an old logging bridge.

Note that the loop trail from Waters Millpond intersects your route from the right in the southwest corner of the meadow. If the meadow is dry it is not too difficult to search for the start, and in winter, there is no problem. In summer, finding the trail's beginning can be difficult.

Beyond the meadow the trail to Dexter Lake heads a little west of north for ⅛ mile and then swings to a northeasterly course, climbing part way up a small hill. The next mile is one of the prettiest sections, for it passes through a stand of huge, straight

Tea kettle at the old logging camp on Knapps Long Lake

maples on the slopes of the hill. Here the trail contours around the hillside. Next it swings north to avoid the swamps that surround the outlet of Dexter Lake and then east to a meadow by the lake's outlet. A few rocks in the clearing mark out foundations of a small settlement, and some stones placed across the outlet indicate a manmade crossing or dam. Apple trees in the natural meadow at the outlet suggest that the site was inhabited for a period of time.

Remote and pretty, Dexter is a favorite lake with many and a desirable camping location. The northern shores are gently sloping and dry. The lake is the hub of several routes, and although all are long (this one is the shortest), they are easy to walk and ski.

47 Knapps Long Lake
Path along old road; hiking,
cross-country skiing, snowshoeing

Knapps Long Lake lies about ⅔ mile west of Dexter Lake (section 46). There used to be a marked snowmobile trail to it from the Powley-Piseco Road on the west that went past Knapps Reservoir, but at present its beginning is on posted land. In fact, there is a whole maze of logging roads in the area west of Knapps Long Lake, some quite confusing. Since all begin on private land, they are not described in this guide. However, Knapps Long Lake is fascinating, and might be a desirable destination for those who choose to camp at Dexter Lake.

Starting where the snowmobile trail to Dexter Lake described in section 46 crosses Dexter's outlet, walk along the western shore on an informal path for 150 yards. A path leaves the shore at right angles, following an old logging road west to Knapps Long Lake. You climb a hill heading a little north of west and then continue through a draw between two low hills. Stay close to the southern edge of the draw, below lovely cliffs that range to thirty feet in height.

The path descends from the draw on a gentle, long slope to a swampy area near the northern end of Knapps Long Lake. Mark the place well for your return, for the beginning of the road is overgrown and difficult to find coming from the lake. Allow forty minutes for a one-way walk between the two lakes.

The lake stretches northeast for ½ mile; it is long and thin and full of stumps and little islands, which make it appear like either a

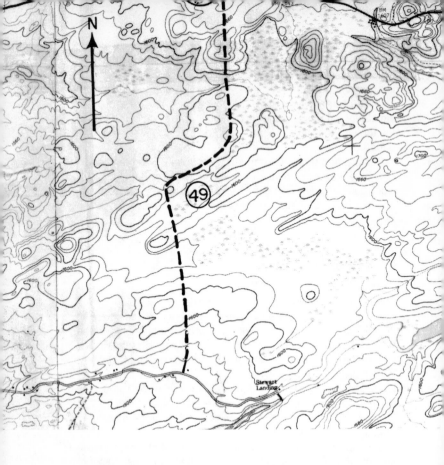

rotting swamp or a romantic wilderness, depending on the lighting. There was a settlement at the outlet of the lake, little of which remains. Scrub forest surrounds the northern shores, so walking there is difficult. The best campsite is by the outlet where the settlement stood.

48 From West Lake past
Burnt Vly Stream
*Path along old road; hiking, cross-country
skiing, snowshoeing*
Another old logging road that provides a good path for walking today runs west and north from West Lake, passing near Burnt

106

Vly Stream and emerging on Route 29A about 2¾ miles west of Pine Lake. As is typical of so many logging roads in the southern Adirondacks, it is alternately obvious or totally concealed by new growth. It would be difficult to follow if area residents had not marked sections, probably to delineate an unofficial snowmobile trail. Look for both red and yellow splashes of spray paint with reflecting cat's eyes.

Since the path runs through a very swampy area near West Lake, it is easiest to walk in dry weather. Plant lovers will appreciate it anytime, for it is a good damp woods for native wildflowers, including the frog orchid, profusions of ferns, several kinds of club mosses, and a forest cover that varies from dense softwood to high, open, and almost mature hardwood. Additionally, the trail is close to the Burnt Vly Stream, giving access to its swamps and beaver flows.

Because of the wetness the 3-mile walk is probably most enjoyable if you take it one way only. If this is your choice, leave one car at the dirt road that intersects Route 29A, some 2¾ miles west of Pine Lake. It leads to property recently sold to the state.

Then drive to the fishing access on Sawdust Creek, the outlet of Pine Lake into Canada Lake. The access is off a right fork from West Lake Road, which leaves Route 10, 1 mile northwest of the bridge between Canada and Green lakes. It is best to leave your second vehicle here as all parking on West Lake itself is private. Walk west to West Lake and take the public trail that passes in front of the camps. At the last camp, enter the swampy area west of the yard. For a short distance the path is all but invisible, but if you continue west, exploring the swamp, it should be fairly easy to pick up.

Novices at walking paths over abandoned logging roads could use this short stretch as a test of their ability to read the woods for signs of old roads and trails, with the assurance that the informal trail marks will keep them from getting lost. At one point, where the path loops north and then turns southwest, the marks are welcome, as ferns and shrubby growth conceal other signs of the path.

The route continues a little south of west, through low hemlock and spruce thickets to a clearing and house by the dirt road on Route 29A. You can walk south of the house to view the swamp before continuing northwest on the dirt road to the highway. The walk should take no more than two hours.

49 From Lake Pleasant South toward Stewart Landing
Trail; hiking, cross-country skiing

A 3-mile-long snowmobile trail connects the Lake Pleasant area and Route 29A on the north with the road to Stewart Landing on the south. There is little change in elevation over its entire length, as it crosses mostly flat and swampy land. Some of the swamps are quite handsome, but the surrounding woods have been logged. This is a marginal trail for hikers but desirable for cross-country skiers. Snowmobile use is so sporadic skiers should not be particularly bothered. In winter, the trailhead, $\frac{3}{5}$ mile west of the outlet of Pleasant Lake, is usually marked and easy to spot. If snow prevents roadside parking, leave your car at the turnout for the trail to Fourth and Third lakes (section 43) and ski along snowbanks beside the road for $1\frac{3}{10}$ miles to the trailhead.

VI
Along the Stoner Trail

Route 10, north of Canada Lake, is often called the Stoner Trail after the trapper who spent most of his long life, from 1762 to 1853, in Caroga Township. Nick Stoner, a major in the War of 1812, did not lay out the course of the road, but he did act as guide to the first party to survey the route. Stoner's biographer, Jeptha R. Simms, enlivened the trapper's reputation with such fantasy that his name has always been associated with the route.

In the early 1800s, New York State was anxious to survey the Ox-Bow Patent, land adjacent to Piseco. The only roads toward that part of the wilderness headed north from Johnstown. Lawrence Vrooman and James McLallin were commissioned in 1810 to survey an extension through Caroga to Piseco, and Nick Stoner was the guide for the survey party. That road was never built, and it was not until 1841, after a second survey, that a road was constructed along the route drawn by the 1810 party.

Simms's *Trappers of New York,* written in 1850, tells of many of Stoner's adventures on the lakes and streams near the road. Simms described this section of the wilderness as having "a primeval look. Its majestic forest lords and advantageous water powers must in time invite a thrifty artisan and hardfisted yeoman to subdue and cultivate it. It abounds in waters the most limpid, and breezes most invigorating. The lakes and their tributaries are stored with an abundance of delicious trout; and if not walled castles, stately mansions may yet rear their imposing fronts in these glens; to be known in future ages as the rivals of the far-famed glens of Scotland." How surprised Simms might be to discover that parts of the wilderness are as wild and untamed as when he first saw them.

The Stoner Lakes, called the Stink Lakes by Stoner and his

companions, are the most northern of the lakes that drain into Canada Lake. The section of Route 10 that roughly parallels the Stoner Lake outlet, from Pine Lake to the Stoner Lakes, holds the half dozen adventures described in sections 50 through 56.

50 Broomstick Lake

Trail; hiking, picnicking,
camping, fishing, snowshoeing,
cross-country skiing

The traditional route to Broomstick Lake, along an old roadway, is now a snowmobile trail. It is so short, however, that snowmobiles rarely use it and so well defined and marked that it makes a good winter trek for novice snowshoers or cross-country skiers. Hikers the rest of the year will also find the route worth taking, for there is much to see along the way.

The trail begins on the west side of Route 10, just 1$\frac{1}{10}$ miles north of Pine Lake. Over the $\frac{2}{3}$-mile distance to Broomstick Lake, you climb only 300 feet, so the grade is barely noticeable.

You proceed a little south of west for about half the distance and then head more to the north, where the trail curves along the shallow ravine through which the Broomstick Lake outlet flows. Here, beside the trail, you can find many native wildflowers that are distinctive of the deep woods, including pink Lady's slippers in spring and rattlesnake orchids in midsummer.

The trail crosses the head of the peculiar ravine and then passes through a small ferny meadow, a stretch of woods, and finally a swampy area just below the beaver dam at the foot of the lake. The swamp is full of bottled gentian in August. If you cross the dam to the eastern shore you will find a charming camping spot under hemlocks and one of the southernmost stands of Labrador tea in the Adirondacks.

Broomstick Lake was erroneously named Goose Egg on some of the early maps, but it is not evident that either name fits its shape. One of the more interesting historical notes connected with the lake is that one of the earliest movies ever made, the silent film *Last of the Mohicans,* was filmed on its shores. At least one resident of Canada Lake still recalls playing the role of an Indian in the film. A stockade was erected on the promontory that is now the lake's best campsite.

The story of the ravine beside the trail is curious. Rumors persist that it was created by a gigantic explosion that was part of another movie script done by the same producers, Blazed Trail Productions. It certainly does not appear to be a natural feature, but its real history may never be known.

Broomstick Lake is a very desirable destination for snowshoers. Expert winter travelers, those who need no trail, may enjoy reaching it by way of a 3-mile-long bushwhack loop off the marked route. The bushwhack and return by trail takes about four hours to snowshoe, which leaves time enough for a picnic.

For the bushwhack, follow the Broomstick Lake trail about ¼ mile, until it swings north. At that point, leave the trail and head west-southwest through the draw formed by two small hills, toward the north end of Nine Corner Lake. The northern hill borders the lake, and the natural draw to its south makes an easily defined route for the cross-country trek. When you reach Nine Corner Lake, walk out to the islands in the northern lobe, which provide a hemlock- and spruce-covered shelter for a picnic. From the islands head north up the ridge of the hill; the route is relatively steep but will take you past ledges with winter outlooks and views of Lily Lake and the Canada Lake outlet. From the outlook just below the crest, head 40 degrees east of magnetic north to Broomstick Lake, using the northeast slopes of the hill to guide you. Cross the lake to the beaver dam at the outlet and enjoy exploring the frozen vly below it, usually a photogenic spot in winter. Then follow the snowmobile trail back to your start on Route 10.

Of course, you must be adept at using a map and compass for the bushwhack route described. Nine Corner Lake lies in a band of extremely heavy winter snows. Snow of great depth, often over four feet, persists through March, so a snowshoe trek is still possible here when the weather becomes a little milder, precluding trips elsewhere.

51 Stoner Lake Outlet
Picnic spots; picnicking

There are several picnic spots of real beauty along Route 10 on the Stoner Lake outlet. At the first, 1 mile north of Pine Lake, cardinal flowers bloom in August beside the stream, not 50 feet from the road. One-tenth mile farther north, just opposite the

Stoner Lake Gorge

Broomstick Lake trailhead, there is a parking place beside the stream, and room for both picnicking and camping.

The best place of all is the Stoner Lake Gorge, 2½ miles north of Pine Lake. Stretching ¼ mile below the outlet of East Stoner Lake, the seemingly remote beauty of the spot belies its proximity to the road. For those who cannot trek to distant gorges, there is no more beautiful place. A series of small falls and deep ledges make it an artist's delight. It is an especially deep, cool, and dark place on a warm sunlit day. In fact, it is so dark it will frustrate photographers, who will find early spring the only time when the gorge is well lighted.

52 West Stoner Lake to Good Luck Lake

Trail; cross-country skiing

The route from West Stoner Lake to Good Luck Lake has the distinction of being called the "military road" by some area residents, who believe that it served as a martial route in some war. It certainly was a logging road and at one time part of the principal road north, but no evidence of its military significance has ever been found.

The route has been marked by the DEC as a snowmobile trail and gives access to several interesting loops. The trail may be too wet and dull to attract summer hikers; however, it has great potential for ski touring. To find the southern end of the trail, drive or ski west from Route 10 along the North Shore Road of West Stoner Lake for ½ mile. Your mode of travel will depend on whether the road has been plowed or not.

The trail heads northwest from North Shore Road between West Lake Mountain and Rooster Hill and crosses the marked Route 10-Third Lake snowmobile trail (section 53) in just ¾ mile. Natives call this intersection "the four corners." Continue straight across. In the next 1¼ miles the path is flat and occasionally wet, crossing four streams before intersecting the Good Luck Lake-Spectacle Lake snowmobile trail a litle over ¼ mile from the southwest corner of Good Luck Lake.

Again continuing straight across the intersection, the trail skirts the vlies that lie southeast of Good Luck Lake, between the water and the road. Unfortunately the trail isn't close enough to afford interesting summer views. However, because the long, gentle route follows an old logging road, it is perfect for cross-country skiing.

Use this route for ski-touring practice, returning when you have had enough. Or you could use this route to shorten the trip to Third and Fourth lakes (section 53), or to make an extended trek to Spectacle Lake (section 65). Alternatively, you could use this route for a through-trek across Good Luck Lake, if you can arrange for transportation at the trailhead just to its north (see section 64). To do this alternative, you will turn right when you reach the Good Luck Lake-Spectacle Lake trail, ski downhill until you reach the level of the lake, and then cut cross-country through the trees, carefully. The open ski trek across the lake to Route 10 can be most attractive.

53 From Route 10 to
Third and Fourth Lakes
Trail; hiking, cross-country skiing

Third and Fourth lakes used to be accessible from Route 10 entirely by way of an old logging road. The first section of road crosses private lands, however, so when the route was desig- nated a marked snowmobile trail, a new section was cut from Route 10. It intersects the old logging road after ¼ mile. The trail begins on the west side of Route 10 in Arietta, almost 1 mile north of the Hamilton-Fulton county line. The new section is so wet — one time I tried to walk it the trail was under a foot of water — that the best use of the trail may be in winter.

However, if it is not too wet to walk the first ¼ mile, the trail does provide hikers an almost level 2⅔-mile route to Third Lake. The distance can be covered in an hour and a half. The first part of the trail is through abandoned farmland and woods that have been so heavily cut the trees are a short, scrubby mixture of hardwoods and evergreens. You will find delightfully many field flowers along the trail here.

After rising gently to climb around the lower northwest slopes of Rooster Hill, the trail crosses the West Stoner Lake-Good Luck Lake snowmobile trail (section 52) almost 1½ miles from Route 10. West of the intersection, across the north slopes of West Lake Mountain, the woods are high, open hardwoods with an occa- sional very large hemlock or spruce. Beyond West Lake Mountain the forest cover again becomes smaller, indicating heavy and

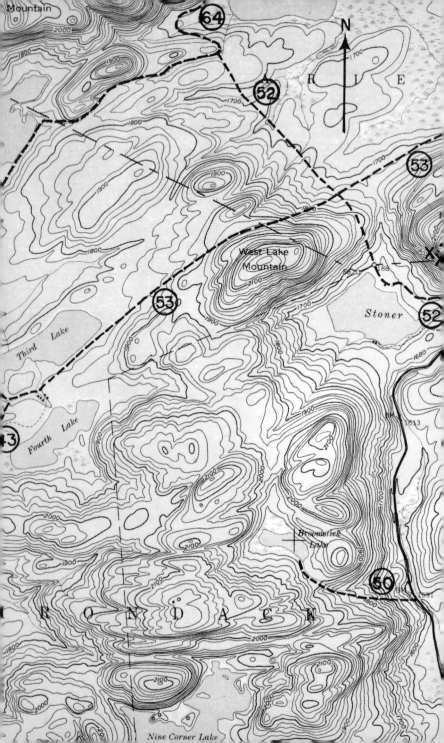

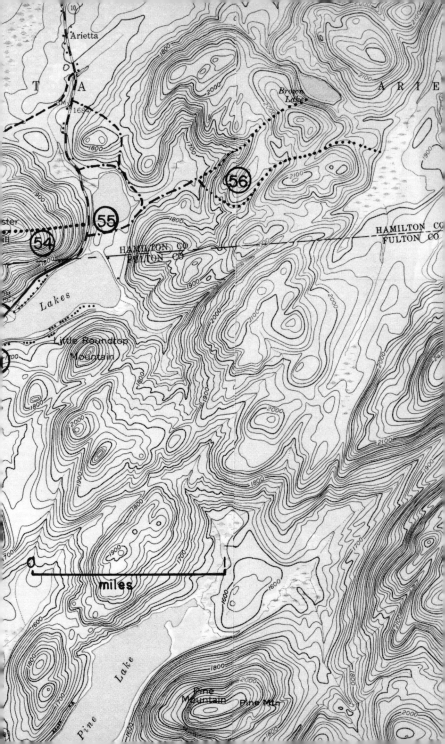

more recent logging. Here the trail runs level for nearly 1 mile, over a stretch that is very wet, buggy and swampy, even in dry weather.

The official marked snowmobile trail ends at the southwest corner of Third Lake near a large beaver house. In winter snowmobilers continue across the lake to intersect the snowmobile trail from Route 29A along Burnt Vly (section 43).

The old logging road does continue along the south shore of Third Lake, and although some brush fills the path, it is easy to follow all the way down to the site of the old settlement that spanned the outlet from Fourth Lake into Third Lake (see section 43). The settlement today is mostly evident by its huge garbage dump. Here, at the north of the clearing between the lakes, you will find a bridge across the stream. It was built before this part of the Burnt Vly snowmobile trail was disturbed by beaver work. This connection gives you easy access to numerous other trails and old roads.

Depending on beaver work, you can walk through the clearing and around swampy ground to Fourth Lake on the south. Fourth Lake is almost a carbon copy of Third. Both are ½ mile long, rather narrow, swampy at the edges, and surrounded by high ground covered with heavily logged mixed forests. Neither has good views of any of the Adirondacks' high hills.

The distance from the end of the snowmobile trail at Third Lake to the settlement area is ½ mile, and it takes more than an hour just to walk that section and return. If you do hike this section, your total round trip from Route 10 will take four hours. Note that the Burnt Vly trail from the south takes five hours for the round trip.

This trail is fairly actively used by snowmobilers in winter, but not so heavily as to limit cross-country ski use. As with the other abandoned logging roads in the area, this is an ideal route for ski touring, for in winter, the lake shores are accessible and even the trail seems more handsome.

54 Cliffs on Rooster Hill
Easy bushwhack; snowshoeing

Rooster Hill rises to the north of West Stoner Lake. There are no paths on it, but it is possible to bushwhack from Route 10 up along its gentle eastern shoulder to some south-facing cliffs. Because there are no high hills to the immediate south, they offer a fine view of the Stoner Lakes and distant hills.

The views are best in winter, and this trip has become a popular, easy snowshoe trek, perhaps one of the finest around. Of course, you should be able to read a map and use a compass, but the bushwhack course is rather easy to follow.

Start at the parking turnout on the east side of Route 10 at the north end of East Stoner Lake. Across the road from it and 100 yards north, take a due westerly course for the summit of Rooster Hill. The climb, of under 500 feet in over ½ mile, is fairly constant. When you reach the summit, walk southwest 300 yards to find the cliffs.

You will be surprised at the depth of the snow on the summit. If you poke about, you may discover other openings with views to the east and southeast, but the views from the cliffs are best.

With a knowledgeable guide to lead you, Rooster Hill is a perfect first climb for those learning to snowshoe. The trip up takes little more than an hour and a quarter.

55 Upper Stoner Lake

Path, picnic spot; walking, picnicking,
fishing, canoeing, camping

The northernmost of the three Stoner Lakes lies east of Route 10 and is much smaller than West Stoner and East Stoner, but it is surrounded entirely by public land. With easy access and lovely shores, it provides one of the prettiest picnic and camping sites along Route 10.

Park at the turnout at the north end of East Stoner Lake and walk 300 feet along the road to a sign designating a footpath. The path crosses the outlet of Upper Stoner Lake; for hikers this crossing can be a wet business of hopping on logs and stones. East of the stream, the path divides; the right, or south, fork approaches the northern undeveloped shore of East Stoner Lake. The left fork follows the outlet north a short distance to the southern end of Upper Stoner Lake and a well-used picnic site on a sandy shore under a lovely hemlock grove.

This is an excellent place to bring a rubber boat or canoe, since the carry is almost nothing. There is another path, but no parking place on Route 10 just 300 yards north of the marked footpath. This route brings you to the shores of the lake in a few feet, so is the ideal spot for launching.

There is also a very good path from the picnic site along the southern end of the lake that runs through a large hemlock stand.

It is amazing that these giants could have survived the tanbark stripping of the nineteenth century or that they could have grown to such size since then.

Many lovely large birch grace the woods around the lake, and the woods floor, softly cushioned with hemlock needles, is perfect for enjoying the typical plants of the deep woods. The eastern or inlet end of the lake has a swampy area with deep layers of sphagnum bog. At the edge of the bog, you will see a faint fork in the path. Take the right fork and bushwhack across the wet eastern end of the lake where it is possible to pick up a path that encircles the northern half of the lake. If you continue along it toward Route 10, you will come to two trail junctions. At the first, a right, or north, turn leads to a logging road that has been cut over the shoulder of the mountain north of Upper Stoner Lake. By this route, it is only a fifteen-minute, ½-mile walk from the lake back to Route 10. You cut through a draw, swing north, and emerge on the highway opposite the outboard motor sales store in Arietta. To circle the lake, bear left and at the second fork, keep left again, because the right fork ends in a private backyard.

An altogether lovely day can be planned near Upper Stoner Lake, picnicking, boating, and enjoying walks and wildflowers along the paths around the lake.

56 Whitman Flow and Brown Lake
Easy bushwhacks; hiking, snowshoeing

The path around the south shore of Upper Stoner Lake (section 55) continues east past the bog. Informal and unmarked, it is sufficiently visible to start you on the way toward two bushwhacks. One of them leads to an uninhabited lake seldom visited except by fishermen. The other leads toward a flow on one of the tributary streams of the West Branch of the Sacandaga.

Walk along the south shore of Upper Stoner Lake, following the informal path and taking the right fork as it heads east, staying south of the beautiful, deep moist woods at the eastern edge of the lake. Hunters have kept the route open with notched trees, but at present the path is pretty overgrown. The path heads east northeast through a valley and is fairly obvious for the first mile. After crossing an intermittent stream, it continues south of east around a rocky ridge and through an area of heavy blowdowns, the result apparently of violent winds as well as the beech die-back. Here, the blowdowns and new witch hobble and bramble growth obliterate the path.

After crossing the ridge, the path descends to the swamps around Whitman Flow, where there is some supposedly good fishing. This route has been used to launch a bushwhack walk east toward Duck Lake and County Line Lake, ending at the Pinnacle Valley Road.

Probably more interesting to hikers is the bushwhack toward Brown Lake. Start as above, watching for where the path bears southeast to cross the intermittent stream. You will notice there are numerous exposed rock ledges above the stream. Rather than turning away from the stream bed, follow it east-northeast, and then continue on a compass course of 45 degrees magnetic, beyond the end of the draw. This route will take you through a deep, mossy, heavily wooded hemlock grove. Climb, still on the same compass course, keeping high ground to your right. Bear a little north to go over the tongue of the hill and drop down, still on the compass bearing, to Brown Lake.

The lake is small with steep, wooded shores and two large beaver lodges. You will not find a rock from which to view the lake easily, but there are several dry wooded places to picnic.

For the return, reversing your compass course will take you back to the well-defined valley that drains into Upper Stoner Lake. Note that this bushwhack is not easy and does require experience with using map and compass routes.

VII

Headwaters of the West Branch of the Sacandaga

West Branch country is true wilderness, perhaps the southern Adirondacks' least-known area. Half the forest covered in this book lies within the circle of the West Branch of the Sacandaga River, and the few accesses to it keep it largely untouched for those adventurous individuals who like to bushwhack.

The West Branch of the Sacandaga, frequently changing its mood and tempo, flows in every direction around the compass. Arising in three small streams from three small lakes in deep forest, the river winds like a spiral as if to protect its interior from intruders. The West Branch flows south and west from Meco Lake and near the Whitman Flow joins the outlet of Silver Lake, which has already made its way southward for 4 miles. Together they flow west to pick up the North Branch, which has come nearly 6 miles south from Canary Pond.

Meandering west 4 miles to Route 10, which crosses it twice in the space of 1 mile, the river then turns north to wander leisurely for 6 miles through a majestic valley. As the road parallels the river here, it can be enjoyed easily at many places by hikers as well as by canoe.

Located on Route 10 on a large piece of private land in the midst of the Forest Preserve is Avery's Hotel, a typical old Adirondack hotel and hunting lodge that even boasts a private lake and game preserve stocked with many deer. The view from its porch across the valley of the West Branch, where it winds and twists through a broad meadow, is as spectacular as any in the southern Adirondacks. Flowing through the longest and highest of the mountain valleys, the river has cut a sinuous path through the silted plain left when a glacial lake receded.

North of Avery's, the river bends to the east past the site of an old Shaker farm, which now is little more than an ugly sand pit. Then falling through the first of a great series of rapids, it continues northeast to pick up the outlet of Piseco Lake in another quiet stretch.

Their union is far from quiet, for as the river turns again, now to the east, it becomes a raging stream. Tumbling east for 14 miles over cataracts, rapids, and falls, it drops nearly 700 feet. One stretch has been designated a "Wild River" in the categories of the Adirondack Park Agency. From the Piseco Outlet east to the quiet of Big Eddy near Whitehouse (see Chapter XI), the West Branch country is as remote and inaccessible as any part of our wilderness. Known only to a few fishermen, this section has a beauty that rivals most other Adirondack streams.

East of Whitehouse, the site of an old hunting lodge that is now a part of the Forest Preserve, the river is within reach of a dirt road that remains the only intrusion of civilization into the region. Here the rapids broaden into a wide, rocky, river bed, innocuous enough in summer, but deep and violent with spring rains.

Below Wells, the river turns again, once more heading south to join the Main Branch of the Sacandaga. This river continues south to pass scarcely 7 miles as the crow flies from the headwaters of the West Branch, thus almost encircling its wilderness interior. Because Route 30 is east of the river, with bridges only at Wells and near Benson, the river is here as much a barrier to the woods it borders as are the posted private lands that edge the encircling roads.

Route 10, the only access to the western part of West Branch territory, is now a smooth, curving, two-lane highway where just a few years ago it was only a bumpy gravel road. But the new road maintains a measure of the wilderness route; a constitutional amendment, which would have permitted a straightened super-highway through state park lands, was fortunately defeated.

Just north of Arietta, where Route 10 crosses the West Branch twice, the "two bridge area" holds a special fascination because of the numerous paths that explore it. But it also has a special problem, for here the different scales of the USGS topographical maps are most confusing to hikers. Out of habit, the southern-most bridge north of Arietta is here called the "first bridge" and the northern one, the "second bridge."

57 West Branch of the Sacandaga/Upstream from the First Bridge

Canoe trip; canoeing

While canoeing on the West Branch upstream from the first bridge north of Arietta is difficult, it permits you to penetrate some of the most inaccessible parts of West Branch country. Park at the first bridge 1¾ miles north of the Hamilton-Fulton county line on Route 10.

Low water could hamper this trip, but so could a cold, wet day or unusually high water and a heavy current; hence the timing of this spectacular adventure is very critical. Wearing rubber boots is a good idea, for although there are many long and lovely stretches of quiet water, there are also several long rapids and the only way I have found to traverse them was to drag the canoes while walking in the stream bed.

One of the worst parts occurs in the first ¼ mile, but do not let that stretch discourage you. There is rough water so canoeing the whole ¼ mile is impossible; unfortunately the path beside the West Branch (section 59) is so overgrown in summer that portaging along it is difficult. And even if you do manage to carry a canoe along the path, it is difficult to break through the brush between it and the river once you do reach calm water above the first rapids.

The alternative is to try canoeing. Put your canoe in at the bridge and as conditions warrant paddle or drag the canoe until there is calm water. Then enjoy a quiet canoe trip east. It is 1 mile from the bridge to the fork where the North Branch joins the West Branch, though the distance by stream through the swampy meanders is longer. There is a small beaver dam on the end of the North Branch, and the remains of an enormous dam 100 feet farther upstream. This once formed a fairly large pond, but at present holds only a little water, so the North Branch is navigable for just a short distance.

There are several small beaver dams on the West Branch that require portaging on the way upstream, but about half furnish a little sport if you attempt to shoot them on the return. With a few carries and a good bit of work, the West Branch is navigable for a distance of 3 miles east of the rapids by Route 10. The river winds through grassy meadows, occasionally close to the heavily wooded southern shore, to the confluence with the Silver Lake Outlet.

124

Canoeing up to the point where the Silver Lake outlet flows in from the northwest is not difficult, but beyond that there is a 1¼-mile stretch in which it is impossible to paddle. Here the West Branch comes out of the south, picking up the White Lake outlet from the north and the Whitman Flow from the south. Curving back again to the northeast, it continues with steep shores and rough water. Walking through the rocky stream, which is mercifully shallow, is the only way to reach the last and most remote canoeable water.

Upstream on the West Branch the river is canoeable for 2 miles, and there are large stretches of open water. From an airplane it appears to be one of the largest swampy areas in the region. Unfortunately, it is all but inaccessible.

After surviving the first ¼ mile, you ought to paddle as far as your ambition takes you, remembering that you cannot get lost and that the return is all downhill! You will be well rewarded by the trip into these deep woods and inaccessible swamps.

You can easily spend more than five hours on this trip exploring the tributaries and enjoying the abundant wild life and still not reach the river's most distant flows. Although it is not an easy trip, it is a great adventure, and you might even be lucky enough on the return to have enough water to shoot the rapids the last ¼ mile before the bridge where you started.

58 West Branch of the Sacandaga/Downstream from the First Bridge
Canoe trip; canoeing

Hamilton County is fortunate in having several long canoeable waterways with high starting elevations, some of which are considered the most attractive in the Adirondacks. I think that the most beautiful level-water trip is the one on the West Branch of the Sacandaga as it meanders northward through a wide meadow with excellent views of the surrounding mountains.

The river winds through the valley from the first bridge to Shaker Place, taking such a sinuous course that the canoeable stream exceeds 10 miles in length, although the distance as the crow flies is 6 miles. With a slight current, barely enough to help the paddler, it is a leisurely way to enjoy nature. The infrequent small beaver dams that require portaging scarcely obstruct the gentle route. Allow between four and five hours for the one-way trip.

For such a long, flat stream, it is unusual that its elevation, 1,660 feet at the start, is so great. The trip can be made in any water level, but a cool summer day with wind is preferable because the bugs in the swamp can be fierce. However, the entire stream is lovely at any time of year. In early summer swarms of fritillaries and red admiral butterflies play over the tall grasses and milk-weed along the stream. Occasionally deer show themselves, and in early August a few cardinal flowers dot the banks and some-times fields of Joe-Pye-Weed turn the horizon pink. Late in summer and in early fall swamp maples and witch hobble give brilliance to the shores.

The trip begins at the first bridge. Between the first and second bridges, a distance of 1½ miles by road, the stream flows almost due west, keeping to the south side of the road. To shorten the trip, you can park near the second bridge and start your canoe trip there or even at one of several accessible points farther north. These require a little more of a carry to launch your canoe, but scarcely enough to matter.

One alternate launching is ⅔ mile north of the second bridge at a flow created by State Brook. The brook is very narrow and shallow, but navigable. Put your canoe in on the east side of the road; you reach the West Branch in only 100 yards. The next launching spot is 1½ miles north of the second bridge and requires a carry of about 100 yards. Here, in the vicinity of Trout Lake, a faint path leads from the highway toward the river. Perhaps one of the greatest charms of the West Branch is that you do not even have to canoe it all at once, for there are so many launching spots that the trip can be broken into segments for leisurely paddling.

Upstream from the second bridge ⅛ mile, you will notice almost within sight of the bridge a small stream coming in from the left, or southwest. This can be your first introduction to the West Branch's second charm, the many excursions from the main stream that lead to other lakes and streams and that make it impossible to explore the entire length of interconnected canoe-able water in one day.

The stream is the outlet of Good Luck Lake and the canoe approach is a good alternate way to reach one of the lake's campsites (see section 63). It is likely however, that a small beaver dam on the outlet will separate the river from the lake.

Downstream from the second bridge ¼ mile the river bends to

Vly beside the West Branch of the Sacandaga

the west. Here the outlet of Chub Lake flows in from the right, or east. Recent beaver work has made the outlet navigable, with the exception of the one portage over their new dam. Canoeing to Chub Lake is one of the easier ways to view the plants that grace that lake's boggy shores.

Farther downstream, the course of the river is generally north through the valley between State Brook Mountain on the west and Trout Lake Mountain on the east. State Brook comes in from the west in this section, although its entrance is scarcely noticeable in the main river's many twists, turns, and backwaters.

If you would like an adventurous side trip, look carefully along the north bank of the West Branch, about 200 yards upstream of the confluence of State Brook. The place is in the midst of a huge swampy meadow without good landmarks. A small stream enters from the east. It does not appear to be navigable, for there are scarcely two inches of water near the confluence in summer. However, beaver have created a series of ponds upstream behind a row of dams, none of which are more than a foot high. The first is, fortunately, only 100 feet upstream from the confluence. It is easy to portage over them and the raised water level creates a navigable course for ½ mile to the east. This unnamed stream drains the valley between Sherman and Chub Lake mountains. There are fields of weathered stumps and twisted roots and logs, accessible only by water. The reflections and images of mountains, sky, and sculptured wooden forms makes this one of the best side trips along the West Branch.

Nearly 2 miles downstream from the second bridge, Trout Lake flows in from the east. The excursion to Trout Lake is lovely, and if the water is high enough, you can continue to the northeast to the end of shallow Little Trout Lake, about 2 miles round trip. The more distant pond boasts a huge beaver lodge on its northern shore. If you look southeast from the northern end of the pond, you will have a fine view of the northwest side of the cliffs on Sherman Mountain (section 62).

Nick Stoner built one of his bark cabins on the bank of the West Branch by the outlet of Trout Lake. He stayed there when he was setting traps for beaver along the river. This site, according to his biographer, Simms, in his book *Trappers of New York,* was the spot where two St. Regis Indians attempted to steal pelts and traps from Stoner. Needless to say, the great trapper dispatched the Indians, but the tale is worth reading before you canoe the river. Actually, several chapters of that biography deal with

128

Stoner's adventures along the West Branch and serve as a good introduction to the area.

Returning to the river and again heading north, downstream, you may be surprised to see cars on Route 10. It is amazing how close the river is to the road in places, but with rare exceptions, the entire canoe trip will give you the feeling of beautiful remoteness. Sometimes the corkscrew route will almost turn back upon itself so that many minutes of paddling yield no real progress through the valley.

About 6 miles from the start, the stream begins a slow meander through the broad flowed lands to the east of Avery's Hotel. South of here you will have seen a few camps along the stream, but north of Avery's it winds around Pine Mountain and from there to Shaker Place passes almost entirely through wild forest land. There is but one reminder of civilization, a few logs from the old logging bridge west of Pine Mountain. It is so collapsed that it is no longer necessary to carry a canoe over it.

The entire river is haven for many birds. In the northern flows marsh hawks perch right above the river. Olive-sided fly-catchers and rose-breasted grosbeaks flock in the trees beside the river and hummingbirds mass in the flowers below. Red admiral butterflies join painted ladies and tortoise shell butterflies in the fields beside the banks. If you are very observant, you will notice that the white admiral butterfly appears in both the northern and southern form with their hybrid, for this area lies in the band of hybridization. Even if you are not adept at recognizing butterflies, you will enjoy the dragon flies and bottle flies of every iridescent shade imaginable that will light on your canoe.

Toward the end of the trip, just before rough water, you will arrive at the site of a long deserted farm settled by the Shakers. The Shakers, who began the manufacture of barrel staves and baker's peels, lived at the West Branch site for less than a decade, leaving by 1820. All signs of their stay are now gone, except their name. Even their fields have been excavated, leaving only a sand pit. The Shaker Place continued as a farmsite for many years, and from 1870 to 1900 it was the center of a large logging operation. A dam at Shaker Place impounded water for the spring run of logs, flooding much of the West Branch Valley.

A dirt road runs through the sand pits that have been carved out of the Shaker site. The road is a right, or east, turn, from Route 10, some 3½ miles north of Avery's Hotel. It leads to the site of the dam, and it passes close to several launching places beside the river. Near the dam site are the remains of an old bridge that spanned the West Branch, leading to logging roads on the east bank. That bridge marks the end of navigable water.

It is possible to leave cars both here and at the start and paddle the entire West Branch in one day. Or, you may want to start from several points along the road and canoe it in sections. If you are planning a through-trip with time to explore all the side adventures, and you want to camp and make it a two-day outing, note that good dry campsites are not numerous, because of the extent of the flowed lands bordering the river. The best overnight spots are on the hill northwest of Pine Mountain.

The current is never so strong in summer that a trip out and back from one of the launching places is difficult. Whether your introduction to the West Branch is a short trip or along the entire navigable course, you will be so pleased that you will certainly return many times.

59 From the West Branch to the old North Branch Reservoir
Marked footpath along old road; hiking, camping, fishing, snowshoeing, cross-country skiing

A logging road penetrated nearly 5 miles northeast into the wilderness from the first bridge over the West Branch of the Sacandaga. That road was actively used during the middle of the nineteenth century. Today a walk along paths that follow its course is an adventure into a most primitive and massively timbered country with lovely and varied water views.

Like most good paths in West Branch country, the most accessible and, in this case the southern, has been kept open by sportsmen. At its far northern end, the logging road has become so overgrown and difficult to follow that the DEC has flagged it as an experimental "marked footpath."

So few hiking trails exist in the southern Adirondack wilderness that the state is studying this concept of inexpensive trail building. Just as fishermen and hunters have for years created paths and kept them open merely by walking the same route to their favorite fishing holes or hunting watches, it is hoped that hikers will help keep open a few special routes. These paths have been flagged, but they will receive little additional clearing or maintenance. They will not be formal trails but will remain fitting wilderness routes. Use along a well-designed route will create a visible footpath, and the abandoned road to the North Branch Reservoir deserves to have such a marked footpath.

The roadway begins on the northeast corner of the first bridge on Route 10, north of Arietta, over the West Branch, right beside the modern parking turnout. A sign directs you east to the footpath. It cuts through an open field, which in summer is filled with field plants, bedstraw, goldenrod, asters, and blackberries, covering the way and often growing higher than the average hiker's head. In spring, before the tangle of plants has had time to grow, the path is more obvious and is well used by fishermen.

This rank growth has for years hidden an archeological treasure. In the 1870s a tannery occupied the field beside the river. Stone foundations from the long buildings can be found right beside the path. However, you would be wise to look for them in earliest spring, for they lie in tangled underbrush and thickets of new trees. In spring you can trace out rows of several buildings and find walls, sometimes over two stories high, nestled against the hillside. You may even be able to find the exit flume through which the acid wastes of the tannery were flushed back into the river. Pottery pieces, rusted cans and pipes, tea kettles, and hinges are all concealed in the weeds. Foundations can be found 100 feet from the highway and for 300 yards along the river. Two hundred men worked here, cutting hemlock, peeling the bark, and grinding it to prepare the tanning liquor used to cure skins brought from all over the East. The tannery closed by 1880. Searching out its remains deserves several hours of exploration, probably more than can be combined with a trip to the North Branch Reservoir.

A second entrance to the footpath has been marked but is little used. To find it, again park in the turnout beside Route 10, but walk north along the road for 300 yards to the area of a small gravel bank indentation on the right side of the road. The path begins on the east side of the bank, beside an enormous and prominent white pine. The beauty of this path is that it proceeds for a time beneath a small cliff that is covered with mosses and ferns, along a small but deep and lush valley.

The two paths meet ¼ mile from Route 10. The path beside the river passes through a handsome open cut in a dense hemlock thicket and descends a small hill to meet the route from the north. They intersect at an acute angle, and almost immediately the route swings to the north around a large swampy area. A small

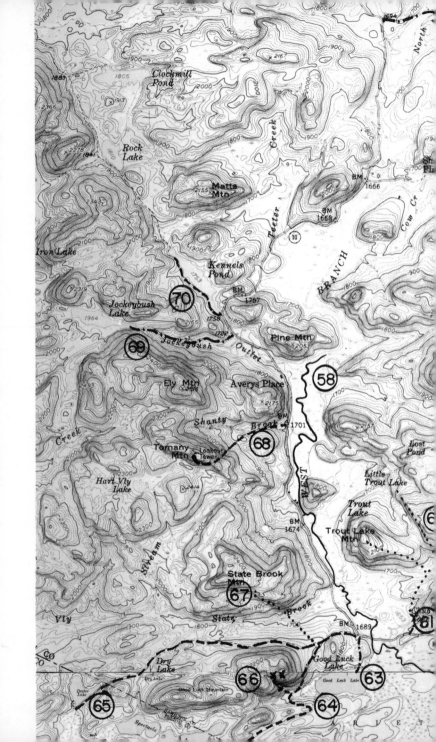

stream in the swamp has been dammed by beaver, and the path is right at the edge of the flooded lands. The beaver have cut some fairly huge trees, and the flow is filled with dead spruce, their bare horizontal branches filtering light to the bleak landscape.

After swinging north around the swamp, the path heads southeast toward the area where the North Branch flows into the West Branch of the Sacandaga. After a forty-minute walk from Route 10, a distance of 1¼ miles, you should spot a fork in the trail. The left fork continues along the North Branch, and the right fork, scarcely visible, crosses the North Branch and continues toward Silver Lake Outlet (section 60). The junction is all but impossible to find.

Just beyond the intersection, the North Branch path swings north of east and for a time follows the stream quite closely on a bank above it. Several old beaver dams cross the stream in an area of quiet flow. About ¾ mile from the fork, and 2 miles from the road, the path comes out in a small meadow that borders still another beaver flow, this one with a fifty-foot-long dam that is at least five feet high. The pond upstream is a foot or more below the level the dam once held, and there is a large beaver house, with no current residents. The beaver flow is near the site of an abandoned house that once served the caretaker of the Arietta Game Preserve. The foundations and a root cellar, dug by Bill Hunter, are still there. The meadow, which has a few old apple trees, is a lovely picnic site and is occasionally used by fishermen as a campsite.

The Game Preserve was one of a series of steps taken by the state in the late 1920s to improve deer herds. After logging ceased at the turn of the century, open areas created unusually good forage areas for deer, and the deer herds became exceptionally large, but then the rapid recovery of the southern Adirondack forests and increased hunting pressure limited herd growth. The Game Preserve, built in 1927, was an abortive attempt to increase herd size. A single strand of wire surrounded nearly 4,000 acres of Forest Preserve, along the county line, then north past White Lake and west to Route 10.

In the western part of the meadow, the old roadway makes a right-angle turn, heading due north and briefly away from the stream. After passing through a thick hemlock stand, it again swings quite close to the stream at the point where the stream makes a large bend. Here the path forks with the right branch approaching the stream and the left one heading just a little west of north around a hairpin loop in the North Branch. This is the closest the path approaches the river between the meadow and an area 1½ miles north.

In the vicinity of the fork and again ½ mile farther north where the path bends east, the roadway has become increasingly difficult to discern. Flagging marking the footpath recommences here, and the route should now be easy to follow.

Beyond the meadow hikers should notice a dramatic change in the character of the land, for the stream is now east of Sherman Mountain and at least 3 miles from any roads, so it has always been remote and inaccessible. There are still signs that the path follows an old road, but the trees are of such enormous size that it seems as if none of the area was ever logged. Birch and maple of such proportions might be expected, but the size of the softwoods is astounding. Probably only the tanbarkers ventured this far, and large hemlocks with a heavy coating of mosses replacing their stripped barks still lie near the path. However, many large hemlock remain growing and I found one recently fallen with an upturned root mass towering twelve feet in the air.

The stream near the flagged section alternates between stretches of small rapids and long peaceful flows. It is necessary to leave the path and bushwhack east to see the water, however, as the path is generally a couple hundred yards in.

Look carefully for the place 1½ miles north of the Game Preserve headquarters where the path again comes quite close to the North Branch. Here, there is a beaver flow downstream and a rocky section upstream, so it is possible to hop rocks and cross the water. The North Branch bends just below the rocky section, and at the northeast corner of the curve a very small stream enters from the east. If you follow it for less than ¼ mile you'll come to Ross Lake, a narrow body of water rimmed on the south with small cliffs. New beaver work has enlarged the lake. This is such a delightful spot that it is worth seeking out the place to begin the side excursion.

Back on the old road bed, you can tell that a section ½ mile farther north was at one time flooded by a beaver pond. Only a few feet from the long abandoned beaver house, it is all but impossible to discern the roadway on the western side of the dry flow.

Old maps indicate that the road stopped at the next meadow, which is surprising in light of the rock work farther north. It is difficult to follow the river here but a short trek 200 yards north through thick brush leads to the waterfall on the North Branch.

The twelve-foot fall tumbles into a deep pool whose western edge was lined with a rock diversion wall to steer logs down the river. The flat rocks above the fall make a good place to stop and rest and picnic. Dark shadows on the pool below the falls make it frustrating to photograph.

Above the fall you can see the remains of a small stone dam. Skirting the meadow above the first dam can be difficult. New beaver work makes even the newly flagged route wet; in fact, the busy animals have created a fair-sized pond.

A spruce-covered thicket conceals the river between the lower and upper meadows. Again walking is difficult, but above the remains of the second dam a long dry meadow stretches north for 1½ miles. The North Branch now meanders through this meadow as a quiet-flowing stream. However, the size of the former man-made flow makes it possible to believe that enough water could be impounded to float logs to the old mill on Route 10, some 5½ miles away. Trout fishing was once considered exceptionally fine in the old reservoir, and it still may be because the falls provide a natural barrier against warm-water species that inhabit the river downstream.

Walk north along the meadow through the dry reservoir. The route is not flagged, but it is easy going in the open fields. Dominated by North Branch Mountain, the reservoir is but 175 air miles from New York City, but this wilderness site could be thousands of miles and thousands of years away.

At the north end of the meadow the North Branch forks. The east fork is the outlet of Canary Pond. It can be used as a guide for a bushwhack route northeast to Canary Pond to pick up the Northville-Placid Trail. Canary Pond is less than 1 mile from the reservoir.

Excluding the bushwhack just suggested, the trip along the North Branch as outlined is 5½ miles to the upper dam and 1½ miles through the reservoir. Any round trip this far requires a full day's walk. There are endless camping possibilities along the way, and shorter trips are desirable.

In winter snowshoe or cross-country trips to the North Branch Flows are difficult only in the first ¼ mile where it is hard to find the path. After that you can alternately follow the path or trek the frozen flows. Be sure they are frozen!

The huge timbers of the remote woods are rivaled only in sections of the Northville-Placid Trail near Moose Mountain, south of Whitehouse (section 94). But nowhere will hikers find a quieter and more distant wilderness destination in all of the Forest Preserve.

60 Along the West Branch and Silver Lake Outlet
Path; hiking, snowshoeing, fishing

In order to reach and walk along the marvelous path that follows the abandoned road beside Silver Lake Outlet, you first have to trek nearly 1½ miles from Route 10 along the beginning of the old road described in Section 59. Then walk 2 miles on a faint road between the North Branch and the Silver Lake Outlet. The path along Silver Lake Outlet is just as desirable as the one beside the North Branch, for it is equally remote, and subtle differences make it a completely different experience.

The entire walk can take over six and a half hours, nearly five of which are required just to cover the round trip to the point where Silver Lake Outlet flows into the West Branch. This may seem like a long prepartion for a one-and-a-half-hour round-trip hike along the more distant stream, but I am convinced that it is worth the effort.

Begin the walk as for the path to the old North Branch Reservoir (section 59). After 1½ miles, you should start looking for the fork where the routes to the reservoir and to Silver Lake split. There are several blazes at the fork, including a very new V, but because neither path is heavily traveled, it is easy to miss the junction completely. Note that it occurs as you are following a due east course, after having changed from the southeast around the swamp. If you miss the intersection, you will continue on the path to the reservoir, entering an area of open brambles.

At the fork, bear right, or south. In only 50 feet it intersects another path that angles to your right. I am not embarrassed to say that here, and at several other places where the path enters swamps and grassy vlies, I have gotten turned around and confused, especially on the way back. Exploring for the route on the outward leg is exciting and adventurous, but missing a junction on the return when you are tired is annoying. Note this intersection well.

Bearing left, you enter a grassy vly. Again note carefully the point the path leaves the woods, and then head due east across the vly. The path is usually overgrown. Sight toward an enormous white pine that towers on the far bank. This will take you to a small beaver dam that can be used as a bridge in very, very low water. It is most likely that you will have to take off your boots and ford the stream, only a small hazard, for there is a good gravel bottom here.

The path enters a softwood thicket 15 feet to the left of the dam and continues due east, following high ground. As the North Branch flows from the northeast and the West Branch comes from the southeast, the path actually bisects for a time the angle formed by the two streams. In this 1-mile section you will encounter two problems. The first, after less than ¼ mile, occurs when the path angles northward around a swampy area. You must search for the continuing path that angles south. Then, after ½ mile, a series of downed trees obscures the route, but with care you can find the path.

At the end of this stretch you reach a huge swamp, which presents the biggest problem of all. It covers a much larger area than shown on the most recent maps, perhaps as a result of beaver work, and there is actually a flowing stream in its midst that is not shown on the maps either.

Walking north around the swamp is impossible, for the going through spruce is too rough. Furthermore, at the end of the detour it is difficult to find the continuing path. Instead, cross the swamp by the most direct route. Fishermen with boots have no qualms. Use downed logs and stumps to cross the sphagnum bog, though you will probably sink in places. You will need a log to cross the stream because the bottom is too mucky for walking.

Fortunately, this is the last peril you will encounter, and the path on the east side of the swamp is much more open and easy to follow. The width of the logging road the path still follows is visible at times. Corduroy and stone improvements make it appear the road could not date back to the turn of the century. The path enters a dry meadow, ½ mile farther east, which is easy to traverse if you keep to the northern side.

I have experimented with an alternate approach to reach this point. Cross the beaver dam at the old Game Preserve Headquarters (section 59), and then bushwhack southeast to intersect the road. If you cross the point of high ground and head far enough east before reaching the road, you may be able to avoid the troubles listed above. It is not an easy bushwhack, but for those who are comfortable with map and compass, it may be the best route.

It is easy to find where the route continues north of the meadow, close to Silver Lake Outlet. A narrow but visible footpath parallels the outlet north for 1¼ miles. It is even possible to follow the stream beyond that point without benefit of path.

The steep mountain to the east and the beautiful stream make this the most pleasant part of the walk. There are several small islands, heavily wooded, in the southern, quiet part of the stream, but farther north where the outlet is narrower and rocky, it tumbles nearly 200 feet through the deep valley beside White Lake Mountain. It is a rare joy to follow the path until it disappears along the small cascades of this remote and unspoiled stream.

So beautiful are these woods that you may wish for a continuing path. If you like to bushwhack, the outlet can serve to guide you north and east to Silver Lake and the Northville-Placid Trail. Several old maps seem to indicate that there were trails east along the West Branch from the meadow where Silver Lake Outlet joins the river. I have found none, and sportsmen who know the area also say they know of none that exist today.

61 Chub Lake
Path; walking, canoeing

There are many intriguing swamps and bogs in the West Branch region and exploring them is a special kind of madness. After all, how many people enjoy mucking about in deep, muddy ooze or challenging the support of a thick layer of sphagnum bog that extends over deep water and literally quakes with every step? But a true quaking bog is a source of great wonder because of the special range of plants and animals that are able to adapt to the relatively sterile environment. This area contains several true quaking bogs, all with the typical plant life, and some are quite accessible. Perhaps the prettiest and easiest to reach, and the one I think of as the classic example of bog life, is Chub Lake.

The lake lies on the north side of Route 10 between the two bridges over the West Branch. There is a good but unmarked path to it from the road, 5¾ miles north of Pine Lake. Using closer landmarks as guides, it is less than 1 mile north of the first bridge and 1/10 mile south of the parking turnout between the first and second bridges.

Even walking the path to the lake is special because of the range of deep, moist woods plants that line the route. The path is about ⅛ mile long, and leads directly to the lake. An informal path continues along the shore to the east, or right.

The bog itself, which lies mostly on the east and north sides of the lake, is composed of thick layers of sphagnum moss upon which grow wild cranberries; bog rosemary; two carnivorous plants, the pitcher plant and sundew; and two native orchids, the grass pinks and rose pogonia. Perhaps you will spot a small grey butterfly, the bog copper, which is found only in swamps. Chub Lake has both yellow and purple bladderwort, pale blue lobelia, bog wool, and the fairylike stalks of swamp candles. The swampy borders host a profusion of woody plants such as bog rosemary and sheep laurel as well as the tamarack and swamp maples.

One large rock stands out on the northeast shore; it is a good picnic spot. An informal path around the south and east end of the lake leads beside some of the sphagnum bogs and eventually arrives at the rock, but the route is occasionally obscured by the dense growth of the wet woods that edge the lake.

Because the path to the lake is so short, it is easy to carry a canoe in for exploring the boggy shores. Recent beaver activity on the outlet has also made it possible to paddle the short distance in from the West Branch (section 58). The beaver have raised the level of the lake so that some of the sphagnum mats are flooded.

Wear rubber boots or old sneakers and plan on getting wet, as this is the best way to see the tiny bog plants. Do walk carefully so as not to disturb them or step through a hole in the bog. And, do not forget a camera and a wildflower identification book.

Chub Lake Mountain lies east of the lake and the cliffs near its summit offer a limited view of surrounding mountains, among them Good Luck, State Brook, and Sherman. The trailless cliffs face the western ridge of the summit of Chub Lake Mountain, which is covered with a thick stand of hemlock and little undergrowth so a thick cushion of needles paves the forest floor near the cliff top.

A bushwhack of a little more than ½ mile and a half-hour's walk from Route 10 leads to these cliffs. Start on the path to the lake, and walk east around it, leaving the informal path when it turns north to follow the lakeshore. Bushwhack east or just a little north or east. This way you will be walking with the cliffs on your left or north, but you will be climbing almost the steepest and most direct route to the summit of the small hill. The cliffs are just below the summit and to its west.

Chub Lake

62 Sherman and
Trout Lake Mountains
Bushwhacks; snowshoeing

As you drive north from Pine Lake along Route 10 you will see a handsome meadow on the north side of the road within sight of the second bridge over the West Branch. Stop here and study the two mountains to the north and northeast; they are the focus for four difficult bushwhacks that offer the best snowshoe trips in this area. All require knowledge of the use of map and compass, and each is a full-day outing.

Northeast of the meadow, across Chub Lake, you can see Sherman Mountain. Its upper cliffs, one of the bushwhack destinations, are clearly defined on the southwest face of the summit. A second set of cliffs, lower and farther west, is hidden from view.

On the north, you see Trout Lake Mountain with cliffs outlining its distinctive profile. These, too, can be reached by a bushwhack. The cliffs that highlight part of the fourth walk are concealed in trees below the mountain's rocky face.

The Upper Cliffs on Sherman Mountain

The upper set of cliffs on Sherman Mountain offer a lovely view of the West Branch Valley, summer or winter. When you examine the cliffs from the meadow beside Route 10, do not let their apparent closeness deceive you. They are over 1½ miles away as the crow flies, and the approach is through rugged terrain. The cliffs are just below the summit, which at 2,640 feet in elevation is almost 1,000 feet above the West Branch Valley. The bushwhack route outlined here is almost the shortest and easiest route to the cliffs, and it manages to pass most of the best features in the immediate vicinity. With time for lunch and photographs, the bushwhack should be a good five-hour adventure.

In summer, begin as for Chub Lake (section 61), walking around the lake to the rock outcrop on the northeast shore. In winter, proceed just east of north from the parking turnout ¼ mile east of the second bridge. Cross the small open field and bushwhack through 200 yards of woods to Chub Lake. Cross the lake to a rock outcrop on the far northeast shore. Enter the woods to the left of the outcrop and continue in a northeasterly direction. You will climb over a small rise and drop into a small valley, which you

View from Sherman Mountain cliffs

143

will follow northeast to the foot of Chub Lake Mountain. The route passes just below its cliffs; in winter their face is hung with great amber-colored icicles.

Continue northeast over a second rise and down into the valley of an unnamed stream flowing from east to west. Walk upstream, crossing to the north side. Choose the point to cross with care, as the stream is usually open in winter. Continue following the stream to the east, watching the contour of the land to the north with care. You should observe two valleys formed by intermittent streams that nearly intersect at the stream you are following. The western one is formed by the foot of the cliffs. You will be looking for the eastern one, however, for it is the best route to the upper cliffs. It is littered with huge boulders and glacial erratics, one of which is a precariously perched balancing rock weighing about fifty tons. It marks a good place to stop for a winter picnic.

Climbing the boulder-filled valley is not easy; the best route is on the east side. A long, level shelf in the mountain face will be your clue to the best way to climb through the cliffs. Follow the level area east to its end and then make a steep 100-foot climb to the shoulder of the mountain. Even though the way seems very steep, this approach to the summit is the most gentle. At the summit, proceed west and back from the spruce thickets that line the cliffs. You will be looking for the one area where the thickets open up enough to provide a view of the valley below. The spot is a cleft in the face of the cliff; from it you can enjoy views of the West Branch Valley with Trout Lake Mountain to the west and Good Luck Lake to the southwest.

From the summit you should retrace your steps. Do not be tempted to try and find the lower set of cliffs from here because the cliffs surrounding most of the summit are too steep for safe travel. Save a walk to the lower cliffs for another day.

The Lower Cliffs on Sherman Mountain

The lower cliffs on Sherman Mountain are also reached by starting the bushwhack from the rock on Chub Lake. A route north-northeast from this rock leads to the valley between Sherman and Trout Lake mountains. Walk up the north side of the valley keeping back from the edge of the cliffs as they develop. The going is rough near the cliff edges, and the spruce thickets can seem impenetrable. There are two or three places with views, but the best is farther north along the range of cliffs. This vantage has views of Little Trout Lake. This bushwhack is very difficult; although the route is shorter both in length and ascent than the one to the upper cliffs, it requires almost as much time to complete the round trip. You will walk over 3 miles and climb 600 feet.

Below Trout Mountain Cliffs

A marvelous winter trip can be devised that brings you past the cliffs on Trout Lake Mountain to Trout Lake and back through the valley between Sherman and Trout Lake mountains. The end of the trip will take you below the lower cliffs described above, and the beginning will take you by some wonderful ice formations on the face of Trout Lake Mountain.

The route of the trip's beginning is determined by the thickness of the ice in the flow of the unnamed stream north of Chub Lake. With care and good ice it is possible to go northwest from Chub Lake across a low hemlock-covered promontory to the flow, cut directly across it, and come out under the Trout Lake Mountain cliffs. If ice might be a problem, cross the stream farther east where it is narrow and make a longer trek around the south side of Trout Lake Mountain.

The columns of ice on the cliffs take on a rainbow of hues, from yellow to blue, and the whole becomes a colorful array of organ pipes. It is easy to snowshoe north, curving around the base of the mountain to Trout Lake. Continue north through Trout Lake and its flow to Little Trout Lake. You might enjoy the northeastern shore of the lake beneath a small ledge for a picnic place. Notice that this is the corner into which the outlet of Lost Pond flows.

From the corner of Little Trout Lake you can either head east-southeast to climb over the lower cliffs on Sherman or make your way into the valley between the two mountains. If you choose the latter, pick your course southeast carefully to find the draw. Climbing into the valley is difficult. Sherman's lower cliffs loom above the saddle of the valley. Descend the valley to the unnamed stream, cross it, and head southwest toward Chub Lake and the return. The trek is at least 5 miles long and requires as many hours. The saddle is only 260 feet above the level of Chub Lake, but it is a stiff climb. While part of the navigating is easy, finding and getting back from the valley between Sherman and Trout Lake mountains is difficult, so you should consider the whole a difficult bushwhack.

Trout Lake Mountain Cliffs

A climb to the cliffs on Trout Lake Mountain can be made in either winter or summer. In summer you can choose from two routes. The easier requires a canoe. Launch on the West Branch at either the second bridge or State Brook (section 58). From either, paddle north, stopping where the river makes its closest approach to dry land below the mountain. The climb from here is very steep, but you should reach the cliffs within an hour.

The second way is entirely by foot. Walk around Chub Lake as if to climb Sherman's lower cliffs, but after crossing the unnamed stream head northwest up the long shoulder of Trout Lake Mountain. This route is longer but more gentle than the route from the West Branch landing spot. The 2-mile bushwhack and climb will take about two hours. The cliffs are below and west of the summit, which is almost 600 feet above the West Branch.

The winter trek from Chub Lake is the shortest, because you can cross the lake directly. It requires about an hour and a half. Start as if you were walking below Trout Lake Mountain's cliffs. As soon as you cross the stream, head north up the mountain, then angle northwest, and descend to the level of the cliffs. Use caution near the cliff tops!

63 Good Luck Lake
Path; walking, camping, fishing,
canoeing, cross-country skiing

There are all too few explanations for the intriguing names given various lakes and mountains in the Southern Adirondacks. Rock Lake is obviously rocky, the Mud Lakes usually offer no problems, Sand Lake is sandy, but a name like Redlouse...? One of the few lakes that have authentic explanations is Good Luck Lake.

In his *Trappers of New York,* Simms tells of an incident that occurred when Lawrence Vrooman was surveying near Good Luck Lake. "Several of the party were making a large canoe from the trunk of a tree, and John Burgess, his son-in-law, discharged his gun at a loon, off on the water. The piece burst and scattered its fragments harmlessly in every direction. The accident terminated so fortunately, that the name the lake now bears was entered on the surveyor's field-book."

Good Luck is another of the numerous lakes easily accessible from Route 10. There are several good camping sites on its northern shore, all high and dry, beneath large pine and hemlock trees.

Both the ½-mile-long path in to the lake and the short path across its northern shore are good, open walking routes.

Park in the turnout just north of the second bridge above Arietta; the Good Luck Lake path and a snowmobile trail both begin within 100 feet of one another on the west side of the road opposite the turnout. The southern entrance is the path to Good Luck Lake.

For fifteen or twenty minutes you head almost due south to the lake over the shoulder of a small hill. Several huge, flat-topped stumps along this trail indicate how large trees grew in this area before it was logged, more than fifty years ago. As the path descends to the lake, it splits into several, all going different directions and all leading along the lake to various camping spots. The lake is small, only ½ mile long, and it is possible to explore its northern shore from the path and enjoy the quiet charm of the lake from several places on that shore.

A variation is to continue west along the path that follows the north shore of the lake, being careful to stay on high ground to avoid the difficult walking in the swampy area near the lake's western end. The path really disappears so that a bushwhack 200 to 300 yards long due west is required to reach the snowmobile trail to Spectacle Lake (section 64). To complete a circle back to the parking spot, take this trail, which follows an old logging road but has been recently recut as a snowmobile trail. Turn right, or north, and continue ½ mile to the intersection with the Dry Lake snowmobile trail (section 65). Bear right, or east, and walk another ½ mile to complete the circle. This nearly 2-mile-long route requires an hour and a half to travel.

Most of the upland lakes are more fun when explored by boat, but the arduous portages required to put a canoe on them outweigh the advantages. Good Luck Lake is a delightful exception. And, of course, it is much easier to camp on the north shore if you can bring in a pack by boat.

To reach the lake by water, put a canoe in the West Branch beside the second bridge where there is a good launching site. Although this trip can be made in fairly low water, it would be enhanced by recent rainfall.

Paddle upstream, or south, for 300 yards. Just before the stream heads to the east you should look for a small stream flowing in from the south through a swampy area. Weeds occasionally obscure the stream's mouth; in fact, sometimes it is hardly visible at all. The outlet of Good Luck Lake is narrow, but navigable, winding through the swamp with perhaps one or two small portages over the remains of beaver dams, depending on the water level.

From the water you will be aware of the significant pines among the hemlock on the north shore. Tamarack fill the swamps on the south and east.

It is also about ½ mile this way to Good Luck Lake. You may see ducks in the weed beds on the southeastern shores of the lake.

64 Spectacle Lake
Trail along old road; hiking, camping, fishing, cross-country skiing, snowshoeing

Spectacle Lake was obviously named for its lobes, which suggest a pair of eyeglasses. However, the first surveyors must have failed to discover all of the lake's circular recesses or else had in mind a many-eyed monster outfitted with a very peculiar pair of spectacles. A deep, evergreen-covered peninsula separates the two largest lobes, and smaller peninsulas and islands define numerous others.

Spectacle's shores are so swampy and difficult to walk through — there is no path around the circumference — that the best way to explore the 1½-mile-long chain of small lakes and bays is on skis or snowshoes in winter or from a boat or canoe in summer. In fact, this is perhaps one of the more disappointing lakes for hikers, because the shores are so swampy and so little of it can be seen at one time. Although there are snowmobile trails on all sides of the lake (see also sections 44, 53, and 65), all but one are well back from the shore. The only close approach by trail is at the easternmost corner.

With a boat, though, you can appreciate the quiet water and explore the coves and bays for ducks and loons as well as fish for the warm-water species that inhabit the lake. A lovely series of little falls marks the outlet of Dry Lake into the western end of Spectacle. It would be impossible to see if you couldn't paddle to the stream and then walk up along it.

Camping here at the end of a day of canoeing is among the most desirable ways to enjoy this distant lake. The very long, thin peninsula that divides the middle from the eastern lake is high and dry. Its good evergreen cover shelters the best camping sites on the lake, although there are several other decent spots, including some on the northeast shore of the easternmost lobe.

Because all of the routes to the lake are over 3 miles long, you may wish to use the canoe trip into Good Luck Lake (section 63) to shorten the carry. In that lake, head for the southwest corner, staying just to the east of the two small inlet streams there to avoid swamps. The bushwhack from the shore to the Spectacle Lake snowmobile trail is probably shortest from this spot. Pick a course south-southwest near the stream, crossing it where it bends west, to find the trail. Cutting through the woods this way, a distance of less than ¼ mile, eliminates over 1½ miles of trail portaging and brings you to a spot on the trail about 1½ miles from Spectacle.

The most direct land route to Spectacle Lake is along the snowmobile trail described here. Park at the turnout north of the second bridge on Route 10. This is the same access you would use for Good Luck Lake. The trail, which follows an old roadbed, is the northernmost of the two entrances opposite the parking turnout. The trail heads west for just under ½ mile to a four-way intersection with a trail registration booth. The right fork is marked "Avery's," the route straight ahead goes to Dry and Dexter lakes (section 65), and your route to Spectacle Lake is the left fork.

Beyond the intersection, the Spectacle Lake trail bears a little west of south for ¾ mile, passing close enough to Good Luck Lake so that it is visible through the trees. It climbs a small rise to descend and cross a stream, climbs a small hill and makes a big loop to the west around a swamp, crossing a second stream, and finally heads south to another small stream. As the trail climbs the small hill on the far side of this stream, headed south, it intersects the newly marked snowmobile trail that turns south around

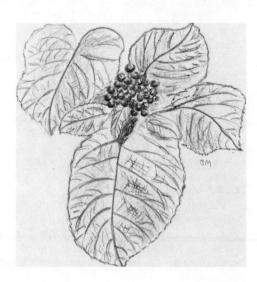

Witch hobble

149

Turtle head

Good Luck Lake (see section 52). The right fork is the route west to Spectacle Lake. Finally, the trail turns a little south of west to follow a draw toward the lake. After completing an *S* curve, the trail pursues an up-and-down course over rolling terrain the last 1¼ mile stretch to Spectacle Lake. A thick hemlock forest edges the trail. The distance from Good Luck to Spectacle is 1¾ miles, and the total distance from Route 10 is nearly 3 miles.

The snowmobile trail continues following the old road bed, heading southwest along the eastern shores of Spectacle Lake. Any walk along the old road bed on the south shore passes too close to the lake's marshes and swamps for good hiking.

That extension southwest turns almost due south to intersect the trail from Third Lake (section 44) ⅝ mile south of Spectacle Lake and about the same distance north of Third Lake. The arm of the Y that heads northwest from the intersection is the snowmobile trail described in section 65 that continues on to Dry and Dexter lakes.

The trail along the road bed from Route 10 is perfectly suited to cross-country skiing and is maintained well enough to be recommended. You can ski the 3-mile distance to the lake in under two hours. The hillocks along the trail east of the lake offer little challenge. Ski past the two peninsulas to the boulder island in the distant lobe and explore some of the bays there. You will find a giant boulder sitting in the last bay. Be sure to look back northeast to the cliffs on Good Luck Mountain. A trip up the lake and back adds a minimum of 3 miles to the trek, so the 9-mile outing this provides is a long day's work. You can, of course, cut across the lake's frozen surface at any point and make a great circuit using the other snowmobile trails in the area. Even on a weekend, you will probably not meet more than a couple snowmobiles — and chances are you will have this distant lake all to yourself.

On your return, you would enjoy leaving the Spectacle Lake snowmobile trail at its closest approach to Good Luck Lake. Ski across the lake toward its outlet and follow the northern shore of the outlet and the West Branch back to Route 10, coming out within 100 yards of your car. This variation does not shorten the trip, but it eliminates some climbing. It is really a pretty addition to the ski trek.

65 Dry and Dexter Lakes and Spectacle Lake from the West

Trail along old road; hiking, cross-country skiing, snowshoeing

This route provides a good 3½-mile walk to Dry and Dexter lakes and a better than 4-mile walk to Spectacle Lake. Because the trail follows an old logging road on level ground most of the way, it is not difficult to walk. Both Dry and Dexter are handsome little lakes with steep shores. Dexter can also be reached from the west (see section 46) or by way of Spectacle Lake.

The snowmobile trail to Dry and Dexter lakes is most attractive in winter, either on skis or snowshoes. The trail to Dry is one of the finest routes for cross-country skiing. If you continue on to Spectacle, either on skis or snowshoes, you can cross that lake's several lakes and return via the trail in section 64. This way you will see the best of Spectacle as well as Dry and Dexter.

The marked trail begins opposite the parking turnout north of the second bridge on Route 10. The trail heads west for ½ mile to the intersection described in section 64, then continues straight ahead on a gently rolling course west for 2 more miles to Dry Lake. The trail follows an abandoned logging road the entire distance.

When you reach Dry Lake, walk along the north shoreline where the trail continues back in the woods 100 feet or so from the water's edge, or, if the ice is strong, ski or snowshoe across to the southern tip, the outlet end. The trail continues to Dexter Lake from the southwestern end of Dry, 150 yards north of the outlet. It bears south of west through a draw for ½ mile, descending nearly 130 feet from Dry Lake. There it proceeds on the east shore, crosses the outlet over the remains of a dam, and continues through a meadow to connect with the Spectacle Lake trail and the trails from the west (section 46). The remains of a settlement can be found at the outlet of Dexter.

This route can be used to ski or snowshoe a 9-mile loop that includes Dry, Dexter, and Spectacle lakes, and then crosses Spectacle to pick up the trail back described in section 64. It is fun to go this way, because then you can stop by the boulder island in Spectacle and explore that lake's islands and peninsulas. The descent into Dexter Lake can be steep for skis, but the rest of the trek is moderate.

Another winter alternative is suggested for snowshoers. Head toward Dry Lake, either following the trail or using the valley of State Brook for a part of the distance. Then head south across Dry to the outlet end and follow the outlet to Spectacle. The ½-mile segment between the lakes is especially lovely with a little waterfall on the stream. There is no trail but the outlet is easy to follow. You can head east to the far end of the eastern lobe and pick up the snowmobile trail back, or, if you are adept at bushwhacking in winter, try a route that involves a trek up part of Good Luck Mountain. From the outlet of Dry into Spectacle Lake, walk to the big rock in the lake, then head north up the western end of Good Luck Mountain. Along the top of the ridge there are rock outcrops with winter views toward the outlet of Canada Lake, 7 miles away. From the ridge, cross the mountain heading northeast and intersect the snowmobile trail again. The climb from Spectacle to the ridge is almost 500 feet, and the round-trip walk exceeds 8 miles. It is a very strenuous outing for which a minimum of six hours is required.

66 Cliffs on
Good Luck Mountain
Marked footpath; hiking

One of the most beautiful and unusual cliffs in this region is found on the side of the easternmost knob of Good Luck Mountain, which has a series of small summits. The cliffs cover a part of the

152

southwest face of the eastern summit and are visible from Spectacle Lake. Beneath the cliff a tumble of huge boulders rise dramatically out of a long gorge.

As if the striking view of Spectacle Lake and Third and Fourth lakes were not enough, the panorama from the cliffs on Good Luck even includes, on a clear day, the hills of the Cherry Valley area to the south across the Mohawk.

The DEC has created a trial marked footpath to the cliffs on Good Luck Mountain, turning what I described as a difficult bushwhack in the first edition of this guide into a lovely and accessible hike (see the introduction for a description of marked footpaths). Here, the experiment is half successful. Over the period the route was flagged, a path has worn on the south side of the mountain. Unfortunately, someone removed the flags and some of the tin can lids that mark the north side so that that section is difficult to find. However, the route on the south has been walked enough so that a footpath has been worn, making it possible for all to find the cliffs.

The marked footpath was designed to connect two snowmobile trails. From the north, the route is partially marked with tin can lids, but too few remain to consider it a marked footpath. The approach from this side is thus still a bushwhack. The route begins 350 yards west of the intersection on the Dry and Dexter Lakes trail (section 65). The course is south-southwest to the summit of the east knob of Good Luck Mountain.

The first outcrop reached overlooks the West Branch Valley. The view is better in winter than summer. The route swings south around the summit to continue west along the southeast face of the summit past a second rock outcrop with limited views. Near the west side of this summit knob, the route dips into a small rift and climbs the west side to the best part of the cliff. The part of the path up to the rift is not adequately marked and no discernible foot tread has developed. There is a footpath across the rift to the summit.

The best approach to the cliffs is now through the gorge on the south side of the mountain. Take the left fork at the intersection of the snowmobile trail, heading toward Spectacle Lake (section 64). Just after Good Luck Lake becomes visible the trail crosses an intermittent stream, climbs a small rise, and descends to another stream. Follow the second stream north and west, along the developing footpath. Just below the steep hill, the footpath crosses the stream that emerges from the draw below the cliffs. The small spring here is your last chance for water on the climb to the cliffs.

The footpath continues steeply on the west side of the stream, never more than 150 feet from the cliffs. The lower cliffs often have great ice formations in winter. Needless to say, the hiking route described is a superb snowshoe trek in winter. It is a steep 600-foot climb from the trail to the summit.

Cliffs are visible almost from the beginning of the climb. The valley between the footpath and the cliffs is choked with huge boulders. About two-thirds of the way to the top, you will reach the best outcrop. Here a huge rock slab shelters a small cave and the rock top gives views of the valley below and the cliffs above. That rock is, in turn, guarded by a giant rock spire that looms like the jaw of a prehistoric animal. There is so much to explore in the gorge!

Continue up the path 100 yards beyond the rock outcrop. The path crosses the stream and heads steeply to a saddle below the cliffs. Two hundred yards through the saddle the path turns to climb behind the cliffs and intersects the northern path at the west edge of the rift.

If you make the entire loop, you will find it is the best climb in the southern Adirondacks. It is fortunate that interest in the area has brought about the experimental marked footpath. It is unfortunate that a footpath did not develop on the north.

If you are unsure of yourself in the woods, just walk the trek from the south and back the same way. If you have a little experience with a map and compass, try the circular approach. Either way you will want a map and compass. From Route 10 it is almost 1¼ miles to the stream on the south, the turning point from the Spectacle Lake trail; then you have over 600 feet of climbing in ½ mile to reach the summit. From the north it is under ¾ mile to the turnoff, which is at present unmarked, and about ½ mile from there to the summit. The round trip is a total of 3 miles, and it always takes more than three hours, probably because there is so much to see.

67 Cliffs on
State Brook Mountain
Bushwhack

There is a series of cliffs on State Brook Mountain, some with views to the south and Good Luck Mountain, which obstructs any distant views. Nevertheless, the adventure of exploring the cliffs,

Skiing along the start of the trail to Spectacle and Dexter and Dry lakes

their geological features, and their cover of lichens and ferns make bushwhacking to them desirable.

To begin the bushwhack, take the Dry Lake snowmobile trail (section 65) west for a distance of 1 mile, a good half-hour's walk from Route 10. Then, leaving the trail, head north and bushwhack approximately ¼ mile to State Brook. Cross the brook at the bottom of a short steep bank, climb the gentle slope north for 200 feet, and then head up a steep slope until it becomes rocky. Climb east around the end of the rocky slope and you will be on the top of the lower cliff; its faces are ten to twenty feet high. These are at about the 1,900-foot contour and have no view but are covered with an interesting assortment of lichens.

If you face north, you will see another cliff to the right above you; you can get around and above it by climbing up to the left. This cliff is at about 2,000 feet and has a good view of Good Luck Mountain.

Continuing to the left, or west of north, for several hundred more feet, you will come to still another cliff, this one 50 to 100 feet high with a summit at about 2,100 feet. These three cliffs are east of the summit of State Brook Mountain and 400 feet below it. Contours on the USGS map suggest there might also be cliffs on the small knobby summit, but this is not the case. There are no real cliffs and no summer view, though in winter you can see through the trees out to Spectacle Lake, Dry Lake, Dexter Lake, and across several marshy areas.

This trip is a fairly rough climb because bushwhacking around cliffs is always a struggle. For the return, you can either retrace your steps or descend to the southeast toward State Brook, then bushwhack directly east, staying to high ground above the stream. You will come out on Route 10.

68 Tomany Mountain
Trail; walking, snowshoeing

The view from the Tomany fire tower is shortened in almost all directions by mountains that rise nearly as high as Tomany, so it is not surprising that this tower is among the many that the State has closed. There is no view without the tower so the closing is unfortunate, because there was a lovely vista of the many vlies in the very remote country to the southeast. I always enjoyed seeing part of the West Branch and some of the noble surrounding mountains like Ely, State Brook, and Trout Lake.

In spite of the closing of the tower, the trail to the summit is still open and easy to follow. It is a good hour's walk to the top, a climb of 800 feet in just over 1 mile. The trail begins opposite the parking turnout on Route 10 that is 8⅘ miles north of the Hamilton-Fulton county line. The trail rises steadily west of Route 10, crossing Shanty Brook and then veering to the southwest around the summit. The last ¼ mile is a very steep climb up the southeast face. Winter snowshoers still enjoy the mountain, for snow banks often pile up high enough to allow views through the trees.

69 Jockeybush Lake
Path; hiking, camping, fishing, cross-country skiing, snowshoeing

Several features distinguish Jockeybush Lake from other lakes in the high plateau bordered by the Powley-Piseco Road and Route 10. It is deep and cold, while most others are shallow and by midsummer quite warm. Many are the color of weak tea from dissolved tannins, but Jockeybush is unbelievable clear. The lake is nearly ¾ mile long but very narrow, and it is bordered on the north and part of the south by steep, rocky hills covered by dense spruce and other evergreen thickets.

The path to Jockeybush Lake is pleasant and easy to walk. It is a designated snowmobile trail, but marking and signs are inadequate, so hikers should consider this a path. Perhaps the biggest problem with the markings is that the state has created a snowmobile trail parallel to Route 10 that connects the trails in the south near Good Luck Lake with the trails to the Powley-Piseco Road. The Jockeybush Lake snowmobile trail now shares a confusing trailhead with this connector.

The path begins from a parking turnout on the west side of Route 10, just ⅔ mile north of Avery's Hotel and directly opposite Lake Catherine, a manmade lake on the Avery property. The way to Jockeybush is the northernmost of two entrances.

It takes less than forty minutes to walk the 1¼-mile distance to the lake. For the first ¼ mile, the path is north of Jockeybush Outlet, but after it crosses the stream, it generally follows it to the lake. You climb almost continuously, but gently, for the change in elevation between Route 10 and the lake is only 240 feet. In the last 200 yards below the natural dike outlet, the path is a little obscured by a deep growth of ferns. Sometimes it seems to disappear altogether, but if you stay in the outlet valley, you will be on track.

157

Jockeybush is an ideal lake for a boat, and sometimes a fishing boat is left at the outlet. If you can, explore the far western end of the lake, for there are a couple of small rock islands, and the view toward the outlet is especially lovely. The swimming is very good. The sloping rock on the north side of the outlet has been used for camping.

If you walk past the campsite on the north, you will find an informal path that leads west along the north shore. Sometimes high on the steep bank, sometimes close to shore, it leads to a small promontory about one-third of the way down the lake. If you are interested in a difficult bushwhack, this path will put you almost far enough down the shore so you can head north through the draw between the two hills toward Iron Lake (see section 16).

70 Avery's Kennels Pond and the West Branch Flows

Trails; cross-country skiing, fishing

Kennels Pond is a private lake owned by the Avery family, who for most of this century ran the old frame hotel that overlooks the West Branch of the Sacandaga. That landmark is now for sale, but before its temporary closing a network of ski trails was laid out around the lake. You can still obtain permission to use those trails or to walk along the logging road on the pond's southwest side (see section 13) by asking at either of two houses along Route 10 between Avery's Hotel and the lake. In summer a caretaker can usually be found at the pond, which used to have fairly good fishing (a fee is charged).

History buffs will appreciate the note that Kennels Pond was named for Eli Kennell, originally Quesnell, a Canadian who owned 2,200 acres between Avery's and the Shaker Place. He was the only man who would ride logs through the rapids below the Shaker Place dam on the West Branch. Those who venture into the wilderness to explore the wild gorge of the West Branch will be awed by this fact.

Avery's 7 miles of cross-country ski trails form a large loop around Kennels Pond. The trails were professionally designed and cut to a standard eight-foot width. Four side trails loop to the pond for shorter treks. The area has been logged, but that activity has ceased, and the woods still appear wild, with lovely views of the pond from many points along the trail.

Skiers from the hotel also use the flowed lands along the West

Branch in the valley east of Avery's. No trail has been designated in these meadows, but skiing is excellent. In fact, the flowed lands all along the West Branch are desirable for cross-country skiing. The same accesses to the river that permit easy canoe launching (section 58) are the easiest for skiers.

71 Confluence of Piseco Outlet and the West Branch
Short path; walking, fishing, picnicking

Among the many paths that Adirondack fishermen have carved out of the wilderness to their favorite spots, few are as lovely as that to the confluence of the Piseco Outlet and the West Branch of the Sacandaga. The place is tantalizing because there is no trail along the river beyond this junction until it emerges from the trackless wilderness, 3 miles to the northeast. There, paths from Whitehouse and elsewhere to the east dwindle away (see section 93).

The path to the confluence starts opposite the parking turnout on the west side of Route 10, 14⅔ miles north of Pine Lake. The turnout is 1¾ miles north of the road to Shaker Place and 2¾ miles south of the bridge over the Big Bay of Piseco Lake.

The path heads generally east for ¾ mile, traversing open woods that are dark and damp enough to support a lush growth of varied mosses. These occur mostly over the last third of the way in wet areas where the path is not always obvious. Because it is a fisherman's route, the footpath is narrow and occasionally overgrown (but any fisherman would call it a "clear trail").

The last 200 feet take you through a swampy meadow with alders; the path then turns to cross a small, wooden footbridge over the North Vly stream. The North Vly flows in from the west, and the bridge is less than 300 feet from where it joins Piseco Outlet.

You emerge on the shore of the outlet beside lovely, still water set off by small rapids to the north and south. After cutting through a deep hemlock thicket, the path continues generally eastward, often right along the shore of Piseco Outlet. Like the end of many fishermen's paths, this one takes several different routes, all to places along the shore, the farther ones being less and less easy to see.

The West Branch flows in from the south ¾ mile along the outlet. Both streams are quiet at the confluence, and the banks are

covered with alders so that there are but one or two spots where it is easy to walk to the water's edge. The path really seems to end here, and there is no obvious point where either stream can be forded, even in low water, without hip waders. Both streams have very deep and lovely pools close to where they merge.

This route unquestionably makes a choice short walk. No more than two hours are required to complete the trip in and out, and there are several spots where picnickers could enjoy the tranquil eddies on Piseco Outlet.

72 West Branch
below Shaker Place
Canoe trip

For those who enjoy exploring the West Branch by water, the path to the confluence of it and Piseco Outlet (section 71) offers the only portage route to the quiet stretch between Shaker Place and the gorge area. The 1¼ mile carry is possible with a light canoe. Launch your canoe in the still water below the islands in Piseco Outlet almost ½ mile downstream from the path's first approach to the outlet near the North Vly crossing. The last ¼ mile of Piseco Outlet is navigable, and from the confluence you can either paddle the West Branch 1½ miles upstream before reaching rapids or ¾ mile downstream before coming on the first rapids and first set of waterfalls in the gorge area (see section 92).

There are many advantages to portaging a canoe to this part of the stream. It provides access to a marvelous trek through West Branch country (section 95) and makes it easy to reach a beautiful campsite at the uppermost set of falls. There are trout in the West Branch, but the best fishing is nearby on Moose Creek, and a canoe is almost the only way to reach the stream. It flows into the West Branch, ¾ mile to the south, upstream from the confluence.

The longish portage may at first deter you from bringing a canoe to this point by way of this route, but do not be tempted to paddle downstream from Shaker Place instead. There are rapids just below Shaker Place, and even though it is a simple matter to carry around them to the flowed lands downstream, that canoe-

West Branch of the Sacandaga near the confluence with Piseco Outlet

able stretch lasts for only 1 mile. Beyond, a long series of rapids stretches ¾ mile downstream. In high water this portion of stream would be a difficult whitewater run, and in low water the river has more rocks than water. Portaging the ¾-mile stretch of rapids is very difficult.

VIII
Piseco Lake

The area around Piseco Lake is an excellent place to look for accommodations within easy driving distance of most of the paths, picnic spots, and other delights in this guidebook. Three state campsites, Point Comfort, Little Sand Point, and Poplar Point, are located on the northwest shore of Piseco, nestled beneath the handsome mountains that rim the lake. In addition, many guest houses and motels can be found in the area bounded by Piseco, Oxbow Lake, and Lake Pleasant. There is a fourth campsite, Moffit Beach, at Sacandaga Lake.

Except for the campsites, most of the accessible lake shores and most of the land adjacent to Route 8 in the vicinity of Piseco Lake are private. Furthermore, the best trail on the south side of Route 8, the one to Hamilton Mountain, is no longer accessible from this direction (see section 99). In addition, the tower has been removed and without it there is no view. This is such a disappointment, for its views were unique. Only one other place, the cliffs on Finch Mountain, afford a glimpse of the secret interior of the West Branch valley, and those cliffs can be reached only by bushwhacking.

Only adventures on the south side of Route 8 are described in this chapter.

73 Big Bay of Piseco and Piseco Outlet
Canoe trips; canoeing

If the wind is calm and you are looking for a good open-water canoe trip, you may wish to explore the shores and corners of the 2½-mile-long Big Bay at the outlet of Piseco. You can put a canoe

in at the Piseco Lake outlet on Route 8 or at the western end of the bay where it is bridged by Route 10. Land at the northwest corner of the bridge is private, but there are good launching sites at the other three corners.

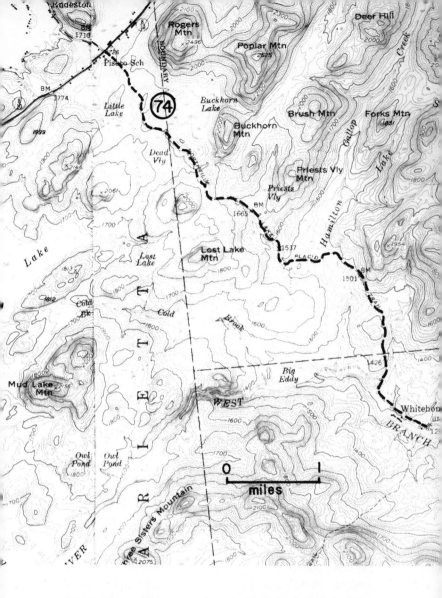

Big Bay is certainly not remote, and because of motor boats it would be best to canoe here in the spring or fall when there are generally fewer people around.

The Bay is so wide, up to a ¼ mile in places, that the views of the surrounding country are not as limited as those on trips through more marshy and narrower streams. Irondequoit and Panther mountains loom to the north, a scenic backdrop to the heavily wooded shores. However, the width and length of the open water also mean that it can become very rough in windy weather. So, while water level has no effect on this trip, wind must definitely be considered.

The entire jagged shoreline can be explored in three hours, and if it were not for other boat traffic and the proximity to civilization, a canoe trip on Big Bay would be considered choice.

A very pleasant day's adventure can be made out of the canoe trip east from Route 10 through part of Piseco Outlet. There is a dam across the outlet just east of Route 10, and there are a few rapids downstream of it, but the rest of the route is a leisurely excursion through marshy grasslands and swampy meanders where there is little current.

Although you could launch just below the dam, it is easiest to portage to the end of a short dirt road east off Route 10 by the bridge and put in on the north side of the outlet. From here the Piseco Lake outlet is broad and bordered with pickerel-weed as it flows in a generally eastward direction.

After almost 1 mile the stream turns sharply south and a small stream comes in from the north. This is the outlet of Spy Lake, and it is possible, even in low water, to canoe up it into Spy Lake. Don't be deterred by the fact that the stream is narrow and winds about a great deal through a swamp. A few small beaver dams also necessitate brief canoe carries.

This side trip provides quite a bit of excitement. There is a very large beaver house near Spy Lake, and the 300 yards immediately downstream have a beautiful, arched tree cover of swamp maple. Watch for bitterns along the shore. The excursion into Spy Lake is 1 mile long, and you can explore Spy Lake or even begin the entire trip from its shores if you desire. The view from the outlet across the lake is of the Echo Cliffs on Panther Mountain.

Beyond the Spy Lake Outlet, Piseco Outlet flows south for another ½ mile along a level course. Part way south along the east side, another Mud Lake flows in from the east; the view to the east here is of Mud Lake Mountain. It is possible to canoe up the outlet and through Mud Lake, carrying over a two-foot-high beaver dam and passing several very large but quite old beaver

Pickerelweed

houses on the way. The young people in particular may enjoy climbing about and examining the huge beaver house at the eastern end of the lake.

Mud Lake has a swampy border, part of which is a real quaking sphagnum bog complete with rose pogonia blooming in mid-July and many of the other typical bog plants. See the description for Chub Lake (section 61) for what to expect.

74 Northville-Placid Trail
from Piseco to Whitehouse
Trail; hiking, camping, snowshoeing,
cross-country skiing

This section of the Northville-Placid Trail is the only route through the wilderness immediately south and east of Routes 8 and 10. If you can arrange to have a car at both ends, the trail makes a good one-day outing — the 6⅓-mile distance into the heart of West Branch country makes the round-trip hike quite a trek. There are excellent camping possibilities along the route, however. The west end of the trail is adjacent to the Piseco School on Route 8, very near the intersection of North Shore Road, and of course, it is adequately marked. The east end of the trail is the parking area at Whitehouse described in Chapter XI.

While it is traditional to walk the Northville-Placid Trail from south to north, you will probably find it more pleasant to walk this segment from north to south, moving from civilization into remote country. This is also the easiest way, for you'll be walking generally downhill rather than up; the total change in elevation is 500 feet over the 6⅓-mile distance.

The trail is fairly level for the first 1⅓ miles to the outlet of Buckhorn Lake; most of this segment is along a dirt road. Continuing southeast, the trail crosses the shoulder of a small hill. After 2¾ miles you will enter the area of Priest's Vly where the trail is again relatively level, but wet, as it follows along and then crosses the outlet of the vly.

Southeast beyond the vly ⅔ mile, the trail passes within 100 feet of the Hamilton Lake lean-to, which is north of the trail. In another ⅓ mile, the trail crosses Hamilton Lake Stream on a suspension bridge. South of the bridge, the trail is again no longer just a footpath but follows an old dirt road south for 1⅘ miles to intersect the dirt road from Whitehouse to the west. Turn east on this road and walk ⅔ mile to reach the Whitehouse parking lot.

Compare the "old dirt roads" of the Northville-Placid Trail with those described in the West Branch section of this book. Foot traffic and maintenance on the Northville-Placid Trail keeps it open while the latter are often overgrown and difficult if not impossible to distinguish from the woods by all but experienced hikers. Both kinds of routes follow level tracks because they were laid out as roads. But, the remote quality of the lesser used paths makes them seem like real wilderness routes. For those seeking to leave the world of man's creations, there is no comparison.

With a light pack, three hours suffice for the walk from Piseco to Whitehouse, but allow time for a more leisurely pace in the interior.

IX
Benson Road

Benson Road connects Caroga Lake and Route 10 on the west with Route 30 on the east, 3 miles north of Northville. It is designated as Fulton County Route 112.

The road generally forms the southern boundary of the Adirondack foothills and is distinguished by the fact that almost all land along it is private. Among the few exceptions in the long, sparsely inhabited road are Pinnacle Road, the Northville-Placid trailhead in Upper Benson, Cathead Mountain, Woods Lake, and Groff Creek, which give access to state land. The land on both sides of the road has been and continues to be logged.

Trails at the west end of Benson Road have been covered in the chapter on Canada Lake. If you are driving east on Benson Road, you will find good views northeast toward Three Ponds Mountain 8⅓ miles east of Caroga Lake and again just beyond the town line, a little under 10 miles from Caroga. At its far eastern end, the road is narrow and twisting, passing through a steep valley with handsome small mountains to the south. It is a rare trip in summer when partridge or pheasants with young are not spotted beside the road. Infrequent traffic and sparse settlement make this paved highway appear desolate. You will use the road to reach all of the routes described in sections 75-86.

75 Chase Lake
Trail; hiking, fishing, camping

The route from the end of Pinnacle Road to Chase Lake is an officially designated and marked snowmobile trail that follows old logging roads. Pinnacle Road is 6⅖ miles east of Caroga Lake and Route 10. A narrow dirt road, it becomes so wet at the northern end that it may not be possible to drive the last 100 feet to the parking place.

As most of the paths and trails in this region serve fishermen more than hikers, it is natural that the only state-maintained lean-to not on the Northville-Placid Trail, is on Chase Lake, reputedly a good fishing lake, Unfortunately, the lake's two attributes, the marked snowmobile trail to it and the lean-to, make it a less desirable destination for hikers, winter or summer.

To add insult to injury, the lake has a swampy shoreline so it would be more enjoyable with a boat, but the distance required to carry a canoe outweighs the pleasures of canoeing in this case. You could even enjoy the long walk to a swampy lake if it ended anywhere but a garbage dump. The area surrounding the lean-to is often one of the worst messes you will find in the Adirondack woods.

A second access is located on the east side of Pinnacle Road, opposite the Beagle Club, just under 2 miles north of Benson Road. This route is used unofficially as it crosses private land. It parallels Pinnacle Road for ½ mile and then swings east toward the lake.

The marked snowmobile trail describes a circuitous route to avoid private land. There are many old logging roads in the vicinity as well as a shorter road that once served as the principal route to Chase Lake. The trail heads up the Pinnacle Valley and then connects with a road that swings back southeast, meeting the road from the Beagle Club access where it heads east to the lake. Either way it is about 2½ miles one way, with two and a half hours needed for the round-trip walk. The trails and intersections are adequately marked, though sometimes these markings have been reported missing. Take a compass and map to make sure you choose the proper directions.

Regardless of the problems at the lake, the walk itself can be pleasant exercise, as the trail passes through high open woods, sometimes hardwoods, sometimes stands of evergreens, with many spring wildflowers and good birding near the lake.

76 Between Pigeon and Panther Mountains
Path along old road, bushwhacks; walking, snowshoeing

Pinnacle Road continues to the north-northwest beyond the snowmobile parking area (section 75) as a logging road. A chain blocks access to vehicles. Walking here can be infinitely more

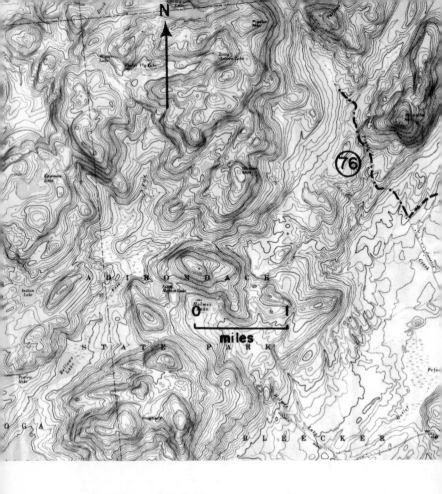

enjoyable than along the Chase Lake trail. It is possible to follow it deep into the valley between Pigeon and Panther mountains, a distance of over 2 miles.

After climbing steeply over a ridge of Pinnacle Mountain, the road follows Pinnacle Creek. There are several places where the creek has been dammed, once by man, other times by beaver. After 1¼ miles, the road crosses a fork of the creek and continues through the valley, climbing gradually. It brings you eventually to a hunter's camp.

What makes a good adventure on this walk to nowhere along an otherwise ordinary dirt road is the number of signs of wildlife

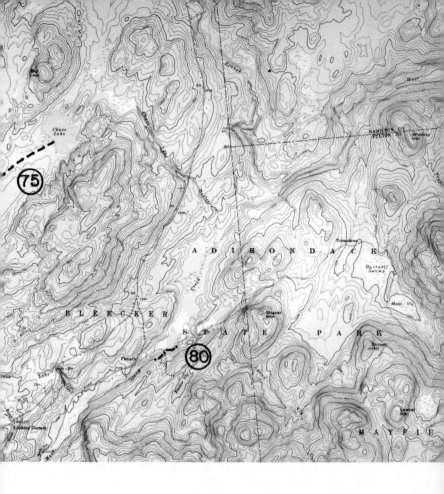

you will encounter. You should expect to see signs of bear —
possibly some of the largest bear paw prints in the Adirondacks.
Allow two hours for the walk and more if you want to do much
exploring.

If you want to bushwhack to uninhabited lakes, this road will put
you within striking distance of the several little lakes that border
the county line: County Line Lake, Duck Lake, Winter Lake, Fisher
Vly Lake, and Little Oxbarn Lake. Fisher Vly and Winter lakes
have swampy borders, but the others have dry shores and could
make good distant camping destinations.

Another bushwhack destination, this one most suited to a trek on snowshoes, is to the cliffs on Pinnacle Mountain. From there, there are views across Chase Lake with Little Cathead in the distance. The cliffs are on the west face of Pinnacle about 200 feet below the summit.

77 Silver Lake via the Northville-Placid Trail

Trail; hiking, camping, cross-country skiing

If it were not for this trail's starting point, I would have mentioned it in the chapter on the West Branch, for Silver Lake is in the middle of West Branch country and its outlet is a major tributary of the West Branch of the Sacandaga (section 60).

The Northville-Placid Trail follows Benson Road from Route 30 to Upper Benson for 6⅔ miles. It is unfortunate that this part of the trail is a road, not a woodsy trail. However, the open route does permit views of distant mountains, which are not visible along much of the rest of the trail.

If you are traveling from the west along Benson Road to the Northville-Placid trailhead, you will come to a sign for it 10½ miles from Route 10. The trail follows Washburn Road for ½ mile, then turns northwest on Godfrey Road, where a sign indicates the trail and states the distance to Silver Lake as 7½ miles. The most accessible trailhead is ⅗ mile farther down Godfrey Road, at a designated parking place and a sign-in booth. The round-trip walk to Silver Lake is 13⅘ miles, making it a long one-day trek. The traditional trailhead, which can now be reached only by four-wheel-drive vehicles, is another ⅘ mile northwest on the extension of Godfrey Road. From there the 12⅕ -mile round trip is still a pretty stiff one-day walk.

From the designated trailhead, the route is along a road that passes quickly through private land and then continues northwest up a gentle rise and around the base of a low hill to the old parking lot by the North Branch of West Stony Creek. From here the trail heads southwest ⅓ mile, to cross the creek and continue west into the wilderness. Compared with other West Branch routes, this seems like a superhighway, groomed too perfectly and traveled too much. The only exception is the West Stony Creek crossing, where the washed-out hikers' bridge has not been replaced.

A mile past Stony Creek, the trail crosses Goldmine Creek. An 1886 clipping from the Fulton County *Republican* refers to a fire that "destroyed the goldmine works." These works were vaguely located in the southern part of Hamilton County. Was the mine near Goldmine Creek; was gold ever really found near here? These are intriguing but unanswered questions.

The trail heads northwest, then continues generally west following a fairly level course to a junction $3\frac{1}{3}$ miles from the upper parking area. A short spur to the left leads to a campsite on Rock Lake. The trail crosses the West Branch of the Sacandaga, here a small stream, $4\frac{1}{3}$ miles from the upper parking lot, and then turns north to continue for a time beside the stream. After passing Meco Lake, on the east side of the trail, it descends slightly to Silver Lake and rounds the eastern end to the lean-to $6\frac{1}{10}$ miles from the upper lot.

The whole east-west leg of this trail is through timbered lands, and the north-south part just verges on the beauties of the West Branch country. It is a handsome but arduous one-day walk, requiring nearly six hours of hiking.

Silver Lake is most often a camping destination. Its popularity has made it difficult for the Schenectady Chapter of the Adirondack Mountain Club, which has assumed responsibility for maintaining the trail here, to keep the area clean, in spite of concerted efforts by club members. The lake shores are a bit muddy for swimming, but its deep clear waters used to be among the best for fishing. The acid rain problem has begun to adversely affect fish life in the lake.

On one of my visits there, we were serenaded by a pack of coy-dogs whose mournful wolflike cries lent an eerie feeling to the lake. Coy-dogs are a hybrid between wild dogs and coyotes. They first appeared in the west-central United States and have gradually moved east, becoming increasingly numerous in the Adirondacks in the last few years. Coy-dogs seem to adapt readily to almost every environment. They prey on deer and small animals, just as wolves did before they disappeared. They have never been known to harm man, but they can be very large and quite startling to see. Although sightings are rare, their mournful and piercing cries have kept many campers awake. They often travel in packs and really do sound like wolves.

The relatively level east-west portion of the trail has made this a favorite for wilderness cross-country skiing, and the trail's breadth makes it perfectly suited for this use. The steep section south of Meco Lake can be difficult for inexperienced skiers, especially on the return. However, the trip to Silver Lake is recommended for those adept at long wilderness treks.

78 Three Ponds Mountain and Helldevil Dam

Difficult bushwhack; camping, fishing, snowshoeing

Three Ponds Mountain lies in the very center of the remote wilderness encircled by the West Branch of the Sacandaga. The route described here is today the only possible access to it. Although the path you take lies along an old logging road, it is so difficult to follow that the entire walk must be considered a bushwhack. In fact, the routes are so unused that this walk should be considered somewhere between an advanced exercise in path-finding with map and compass and a trip for which a good guide is required. With this bit of warning, I will outline the route and describe the problems you are likely to encounter and the marvels you will see. Then you can decide if you have the ability to follow such a route. Remember the entire circuit is 9 miles long, has a 1,300-foot vertical rise, and takes at least 9 hours to hike.

The trip begins at the Northville-Placid Trail parking lot in Upper Benson (section 77). Walk the ⅘ mile to the upper parking area — it should take less than a half-hour —and head north from the middle of that field, fording the North Branch of West Stony Creek, and continue north on an old dirt road. Two less well-traveled abandoned roads intersect your route before it forks, just short of 1 mile from the upper parking lot. Here the Notch Road (section 79), the more obvious path, bears right, and the Three Ponds Road proceeds straight ahead.

You have been paralleling an unnamed branch of West Stony Creek as far as the fork. For ⅛ mile now you cut overland and then cross a stream that flows from a ravine on the southwest side of Three Ponds Mountain. This crossing is near the confluence of that stream and two others; one flows from the southernmost of the three ponds and another drains the Notch.

After the crossing, which is roughly a half-hour's walk from the upper parking lot, the old Three Ponds road immediately begins to climb the long shoulder of Three Ponds Mountain, along the eastern side of a pronounced ridge. Unfortunately, this is where the road begins to fade from sight. Disuse, fires, and blowdowns make it increasingly difficult to follow.

As a result, the rest of the way will seem like bushwhacking. A section of the lower part of the trail was burned in a fire in the mid-

Pond on Three Ponds Mountain

1960s; along this stretch the new growth of underbrush conceals the foot tread.

Except in the fire-burned areas, the trees over the mile past the crossing are generally small, evidence of logging activity within the past thirty years. The farther from civilization you go, the taller the trees become; the lower shoulder of Three Ponds Mountain is covered with high, open hardwood forests, one part being dominated by enormous maples.

The road through this section has a heading generally toward magnetic north. Keep the ridge on your left and the deeper valley of the Three Ponds stream well below on your right. Within the last ½ mile of the crest of the mountain, the road bed describes an S-curve up the steep slopes, winding through an area with rocky ledges on the northwest and an increasingly heavy growth of small evergreens, which confuse the way. About one and a half hours from the crossing, you should be nearing the ridge top. In the last few hundred yards you will have to bushwhack over a small ridge and down to reach the first of the three ponds.

This is a shallow pond with much evidence of old beaver work and an old beaver house at the southwest shore. Since much of the shore has regrown, the beaver cannot have been here recently, but the water level remains nearly as high as the beaver dam originally made it. One maple tree eighteen inches in diameter was gnawed halfway through by a beaver who overestimated his abilities — the tree is still alive.

This pond's inlet is at the northwest end of the lake in a meadow of ferns with fronds over five feet long. Follow the inlet stream ¼ mile to the second pond, which is very small and also shallow with evidence of old beaver work. There are signs that beavers once maintained the water at a higher level.

Both of these ponds flow south to Stony Creek. Just north of the second pond is a divide; beyond it the waters drain north into the third pond and then into Ninemile Creek and finally the West Branch of the Sacandaga, east of Whitehouse.

It is a relatively easy bushwhack northwest from the second to the third pond, which lies in a deeper valley in an east-west direction with the summit of Three Ponds Mountain on the north. At about 2,700 feet in elevation, this is the highest of the three ponds. It is also much deeper and cooler than the other two and quite an exciting place. Beaver have cleared most of the small trees from a wide swath along the steep shores, and they have created slides to the water's edge every hundred feet or so all around the pond. The water level appears to be as high as it has been in any recent time. The beaver have constructed at this outlet a veritable Adirondack Grand Coulee, a handsome dam that is seven feet high and forty-five feet long in the form of a beautiful curving arch.

It will probably take a half-hour to walk between each of the three ponds, and more to admire the dam. With at least three and a half hours already on the hike, here might be a good place to turn and retrace your steps, or you can elect to continue to Helldevil Dam.

The outlet of the third pond is at the west end. You could follow the outlet itself, except several smaller dams back up water, making the going rough. Old maps show a road going north-northwest from the outlet end of the pond to a valley ½ mile away, then west through the valley to the site of a pond created by Helldevil Dam, but no evidence of this road remains.

Instead bushwhack west-northwest from the third pond, avoiding the heavy growth at the start of the outlet's steep valley. You will intercept the outlet where it flows north-northwest toward Helldevil Dam. Cross the stream and walk along the west bank. You'll enter a deep gorge where huge boulders choke the valley. This is a beautiful but rugged part of the walk, and even when you reach the pond you will still have a difficult walk around the western shore through spruce thickets and swampy ground to the dam. It will take an hour to hike from the third pond to Helldevil Dam.

Only remnants of the original fifteen- to twenty-foot-high dam remain. It was constructed in the form of a huge wooden crib filled with rocks. The pond was created at the confluence of two small streams.

Since the dam is not as high as it was once, it is only the new beaver works, which cap the crib and raise the pond level four feet, that keep the pond nearly as large as when the dam was whole. You have to praise the beaver for the way they maintain the dam because this is a beautiful pond, marked with a few dead trees and the twisted driftwood of stump tangles. Little remains to show that a logging camp occupied a site here, only the dam and the name; it must have been a helldevil of a place to reach and inhabit!

There used to be a logging road from Helldevil Dam east to Devorse Camp and then east and south to Benson. The Devorse Creek logging camp was on the north-south route from Upper Benson through the Notch to Blackbridge. All of these old routes have also long since become overgrown, but they offer potential bushwhack routes for exploring the eastern half of the area the West Branch encloses.

A logging road also continued west for 2½ miles past the Hell-devil camp to Silver Lake. You can see the beginning of this road on the southwest side of the dam, and a close friend has followed it in parts to Silver Lake and then out via the Northville-Placid Trail. This puts a 6-mile walk at the end of a nearly 9-mile circuit bushwhack; and the loop took twelve hours of rough walking!

Another intrepid bushwhacker reports an even more exciting variation on the trip to Three Ponds Mountain. His trek, made as part of a camping expedition, took him down the outlet of Hell-devil Dam, which is Ninemile Creek, all the way to the West Branch of the Sacandaga. This requires a minimum additional 5 miles of bushwhacking, but the creek traces a handsome course through otherwise trackless wilderness.

To return from the dam, you can retrace your steps south climbing 300 feet up Three Ponds Mountain over the mile back to the ponds, then return down the mountain as you ascended it. Or, you can follow a completely different route, visiting the "fourth" of the ponds on Three Ponds Mountain, or the fifth on the route as a whole. This fourth pond does not show on old maps and possibly was created by beaver some time before the revisions of the USGS map twenty-five years ago. If the area were surveyed today, the map would show no pond. It is also part of the head-waters of Ninemile Creek and lies a mile south-southeast of Helldevil Dam. The bushwhack to this pond will be the high point of the trip with respect to seeing timber of astounding size.

It takes an hour to reach this pond from Helldevil Dam. Stay west of the stream and slightly above it to make easier walking. You may run across an old log structure, about ten feet long, six feet wide, and no more than five feet high. It is furnished with an old iron stove and was inhabited by an unknown logger or hermit.

The forest along the ridge has probably been logged for soft-woods, but the size of the hardwoods in the area is overwhelming. Birch trees four feet in diameter can be found, and the whole forest of high trees, with relatively few beech, is as beautiful as any you will ever see.

Because the dam on the "fourth" pond has washed out, there is now little open water. The shores are grassy meadows punc-tuated by the skeletons of large trees, a rather strange stump forest in an area that will probably return to real forest in the next few years. Many deer have grazed in this small clearing, and there are ducks near the pond, the perfect habitat for both.

In fact, your visit to all five ponds is a great lesson in how beaver provide open areas for deer and ducks and renew continually the cycle from shallow pond to grassy meadow to forest to pond again.

I related a description of the adventure and shared my fascination of beaver ponds with a conservation officer, emphasizing my lament that the beaver is sometimes so heavily trapped in the wilderness. He said that a few years ago the DEC had the policy of trapping beaver to protect the forests, but that it also decided that dams were necessary to provide open water and restore graze lands. When the department asked him to help construct some dams, he declined, saying, "I told them that's beaver's work."

To continue your return, now choose a bushwhack course to the southeast around the southern peak of Three Ponds Mountain to join the route of the old logging road. The first ½ mile or so across the shoulder of the mountain is in spectacular forest, birch of enormous proportions and such gigantic evergreens it appears the steep southern slope was never logged.

From the last pond to the stream crossing is a distance of 2 miles. Another mile takes you to the West Stony, and ⅘ mile farther to the official trailhead and parking area. The descent from the last pond can take up to three hours, partly because it is difficult to find the road and partly because you've already been out so long. The overgrown burned areas can be more of an impediment on the way down than on the ascent. Fortunately, the funnel outlined by the three streams provides a natural guide back to the visible road farther south.

It is unfortunate that this bushwhack requires techniques that limit it to all but a few hikers, for the nearly nine-hour wilderness walk is unsurpassed.

79 The Notch
Bushwhack along old road; snowshoeing

In the nineteenth century a logging road began at West Stony Creek near the Northville-Placid trailhead and headed east of north through the Notch, a draw between Three Ponds and Wallace mountains, climbing 500 feet in a distance of 2½ miles. For a brief time this road continued north to Blackbridge on the West Branch, with the Devorse Camp about halfway from either end. That camp was also reached by a dirt road from the east that no longer exists (section 85).

The southern end begins on an old dirt road that diminishes gradually to a bushwhack, but an easy one to follow because of the obvious valley route.

The trek to The Notch is a good hike or snowshoe trip. Start at the Benson trailhead of the Northville-Placid Trail and follow the route outlined in the Three Ponds Mountain bushwhack (section 78). When the road forks 1 mile north of the West Stony Creek crossing, bear right. Less than 300 yards to the northwest, this road crosses the outlet of two of the Three Ponds. Then The Notch road bends east to follow the easternmost of the three streams on Three Ponds Mountain, crossing it in ½ mile.

The roadway continues along the stream up the steep draw through The Notch, becoming less and less obvious. If you want to bushwhack past The Notch, you can use Devorse Creek as a guide. The northern section of the road, which is not visible now, did not follow Devorse Creek for its entire length, but rather circled west around Little Roundtop to follow one of the creek's western tributaries. Posted lands at Blackbridge make it impossible to complete the bushwhack without permission from owners there. The through-trek from West Stony Creek to Blackbridge is nearly 10 miles; the round trip between the Benson trailhead and The Notch is almost 6½ miles long.

80 West Stony Creek
near Pinnacle
Dirt roads; walking, picnicking

Most summers in the Adirondacks have several periods of dismal rain and cold, and when the weather finally turns, it is nice to have someplace to walk to clear the wood smoke from your head and stretch your legs. It takes time for the woods trails to dry out, so you may want to know of some old dirt roads, still passable by car but seldom used that are dry enough for walking even in the wettest of times.

The dirt road that passes the South Branch of the West Stony Creek near a place called Pinnacle is one of these. Drive north-east on Benson Road past Pinnacle Road and Lindsley Corners for just under 2 miles and turn right, or south, on the dirt road. This road is just over 2 miles from Upper Benson, on the left if you are coming from that direction. The road comes to an intersection in

²⁄₃ mile; park nearby. Three options present themselves.

First, you can continue walking the dirt road east across the bridge over the West Stony Creek for 1⅓ miles before it enters land posted by a paper company. Much of the property along the road is also posted, but there is such a profusion of field flowers to enjoy that it is a pretty stretch to walk.

Second, you can explore the creek itself. The view from the bridge is inviting, and there are several places nearby for picnicking.

Third, if you are the archeologically minded you can explore the foundations and ruins of a small tannery that was operated on West Stony Creek in the 1860s. The site is between the road and the creek, about halfway between the intersection and the bridge. Most interesting is the fact that it is the only site I know of with remains of tanning vats. The vats appear to have had a stone foundation. They held the tannins that were leached from hemlock bark and in which skins were soaked for up to six months in order to cure them for use as shoe leather.

A word of caution about exploring the tannery site: fallen trees and other timbers have accumulated in the foundations of the vats, which are recessed in the ground. You could easily lose your footing and slip into one of the depressions if you don't watch your step.

81 Woods Lake

Short path; walking, picnicking, camping, fishing, canoeing

Because the walk to Woods Lake is so short and its wooded southern shore is so lovely, this adventure should be considered for picnicking, rather than hiking. The path is on the north side of Benson Road, approximately 13 miles east of Caroga Lake and 1¾ miles west of the intersection at Upper Benson. It begins opposite a small parking turnout on the south side of a sharp bend in the road. There are no markings to indicate the lake or the path.

The path is only ¼ mile long through open woods formed by tall hemlocks whose needles make a soft, cushiony path and carpet the shores of the lake. In spite of much use and the lake's proximity to the road, it remains one of the cleanest and loveliest destinations in the southern Adirondacks, thanks to the vigilance of conservation officers. There are private lands at the northern end of the lake, but the rest of the shoreline is owned by the state.

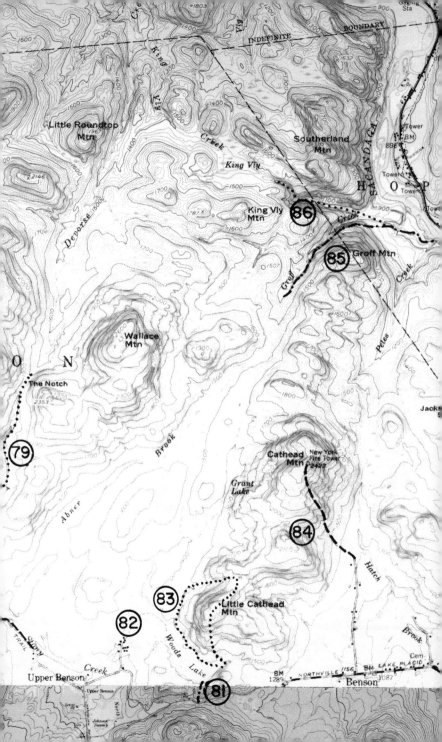

Several campsites dot the long southwestern shore, connected by informal paths. The farthest are free of road noises, which sometimes reach the southern corner of the lake.

The view up the lake to the northwest is spectacular, dominated by Three Ponds Mountain in the distance with Little Cathead rising steeply from the lake's northeastern shore. Because the lake has such beautiful clear water, this would be a lovely place to explore by canoe. The carry is short and easy. And with a canoe you have the easiest access to the cliffs on the west face of Little Cathead (section 83).

82 Lapland Lake
Trails; cross-country skiing

A new commercial ski touring center has opened in Upper Benson on a tract of land that borders on the northwestern tip of Woods Lake. Signs on Benson Road indicate a turn north to the Lapland Lake Center on Norm Storer Road, which is 6 miles west of Route 30 and ¾ mile east of Washburn Road and the signs for the Northville-Placid trailhead. The ski center is less than 1 mile north of Benson Road.

A day-use fee is charged for cross-country skiers, and there is a rental shop. Accommodations can be arranged (contact: Lapland Lake Ski Touring Center, RD Northville, NY 12134;

Across Woods Lake to Three Ponds Mountain

telephone, 518-863-4974). Many new trails have been cut through the woods and more are planned. Nearly 17 miles of trails are already available.

A novice loop using over 3 miles of woods roads connects the center to the lake, where there are lovely views of the frozen expanse and the cliffs on Little Cathead, which seem suspended above. An intermediate loop winds within the novice loop, cutting through a spruce forest and crossing several small streams on handsome wooden bridges. An advanced loop, south of the novice loop, traverses a hemlock forest. There are lovely views from it into the deep woods.

Several advanced loops also range across the hillside west of the ski lodge. Maps for the trails are available at the lodge. The lower parts of the trails are in a deep pine reforestation area, but the upper slopes reach hardwood forests. The trails have been well designed with several good, long downhill runs. The narrow one-way tracks on the westernmost loops are good for wilderness ski touring. The new trail north to Grant Lake, which passes a couple of beaver flows with active lodges, is a real wilderness trek; the round trip distance is 5 miles.

83 Little Cathead
Easy bushwhack; snowshoeing

This is another of my favorite bushwhacks that is most pleasant as a snowshoe trek. The southwestern face of Little Cathead, rising steeply from Woods Lake, is ringed with cliffs, a few with good summer views and many with fine winter views. The approach is via the Woods Lake path on Benson Road (section 81). Walk north along the southeastern shore and then follow the northern shore west for less than ¼ mile. In summer, if you have a canoe, you can shorten the trek around the lake; and, of course, in winter you can snowshoe directly north from the path toward the mountain.

The cliffs lie below the summit and west of it. A bushwhack route almost due north along the long sloping ridge touching the lake's north shore will take you to the area. The best vantage is below the uppermost cliffs, but that point cannot be safely reached in winter. You will probably spot several open places with views, some looking directly across Woods Lake and some looking south to the mountains beyond Benson Road.

The climb is a little over ½ mile long from the north shore of the lake, making the total one-way distance from the road just over 1 mile. The cliffs are about 600 feet above the lake, and in winter you need only an hour and a half to reach them.

A more difficult variation will take you northeast from the first vantage along the top of the range of cliffs to a spot with a commanding view south. Continue northeast across the mountain but below the summit to an opening with a view to the north and Cathead Mountain. You can neither walk nor snowshoe down the cliff areas to the west, but if you walk far enough to the north you can descend through a steep draw. After dropping down more than 400 feet and heading west through the draw, turn to the south to circle back at the foot of the cliffs. You may even want to climb a small shoulder from the bottom of the draw to hug the bottom of the cliffs as closely as possible. That way you will have the best view of the ice formations on the cliffs. In winter the walk at the base of the cliffs is most dramatic.

When you are ready to leave, circle around to the southeast below the cliffs through a valley and return to the shore of the lake. This entire circuit, from Benson Road, requires about four hours walking time and covers a total of 3½ miles.

84 Cathead Mountain
Trail; hiking, snowshoeing

A good trail leads to the manned fire tower on Cathead Mountain, where there is a most impressive view. Mountains on the west and north block distant views into the interior of West Branch country, but the swampy lands surrounding Grant Lake on the west and the vista from there to Three Ponds Mountain give a good impression of how rugged and heavily wooded the region is. The panorama to the east across Great Sacandaga Lake is spectacular. Best of all, on a clear day it is possible to pick out a few of the High Peaks on the horizon in the north and see as far as the Capital District on the southeast.

A sign by the intersection 3 miles west of Route 30 on Benson Road marks the turn north to the trailhead for the fire tower. Drive north for almost 1½ miles and park, being careful not to block either the continuing logging road or the driveway for the private home at the end of the road beside the *very* small parking turnout. The trail, which heads toward magnetic north for a steep 1,100-foot-climb over just 1¼ miles, begins on the dirt road. You come to a cable across the road within 100 feet and 100 yards farther signs indicate that the trail turns to the left off the dirt road.

Take the left turn and notice the row of telephone poles headed up the mountain. The trail runs beneath telephone lines all the way up the mountain. Soon after starting, you will notice a second left turn, which is unmarked. This was a jeep road leading to the top of Cathead. It was an alternate route, as it had a lower grade than the main marked trail. It is now so overgrown it is impossible to walk, but it can still be used in winter. If you do climb this mountain on snowshoes, remember that the tower is, of course, not open. However, you will find the nearly bare summit has views as good as those from the tower in summer.

The trail is direct and steep, in places a series of giant steps in bedrock. The jeep road intersects the main trail in a clearing by the ranger's cabin, 200 yards below the summit. Those last 200 yards to the summit are steep, also a scramble over bedrock. The open summit is covered, in summer, with blueberries and choke-cherries.

There is a spring near the summit. Walk down the abandoned road below the ranger's cabin to the west to a point just beyond the clearing, where the road turns. You will notice a footpath that leads 20 yards to the spring.

The first third of the trail seems relatively level, but the last two-thirds is quite steep. Family outings usually require an hour and a half for the climb. No camping is permitted on the summit area.

85 Groff Creek
Old road; walking

The road along the west side of the Sacandaga River, north from Benson Road, is hard-packed gravel for the first 3½ miles. Even though it passes through private and posted lands, its proximity to the river makes it pleasant for walking or even bicycling. The surface gradually deteriorates, however, and you will probably want to park at the place in 4⅓ miles where lumber has been loaded within the last few years.

Walk the road past here, for a sign advises that the road has been abandoned and that you proceed at your own risk. People do drive nearly 1 mile farther to a camp by Pete's Creek, but you'll agree that the "drivers must have rocks in their heads to match the rocks in the road." Also, all other parking places are posted.

The lands around you are still private, and signs just before Pete's Creek state that both sides of the road are posted. It appears that the owner has also attempted to make the road private, but this is an old public right-of-way leading to Forest Preserve lands. The road traverses private lands for ¼ mile past the creek and then splits. The left fork leads to clearly marked private lands, but the right fork leads to public lands. From here, the Forest Preserve of West Branch country extends in one vast stretch all the way west to Route 10.

After crossing onto state land, the road is only two ruts with lots of rocks. It swings west and climbs through mixed hardwoods around a shoulder of Groff Mountain. Then, in an area of mixed hardwoods, it turns sharply to the southwest, and the forest switches to open hemlock with only ferns beneath. Groff Creek is visible 100 feet down the steep bank. The old road continues high along the creek's east bank with many lovely views, including two waterfalls over ten feet high and several smaller ones. Both the visibility through the trees and the stream's beautiful setting are enhanced by the openness of the hemlock woods, unobstructed by underbrush.

The valley becomes shallower. Soon the old road forks right to cross the stream, and a well-used footpath continues straight ahead. A large downed tree provides a convenient bridge across the stream, which is but a few feet from the fork. However, the road disappears after ¼ mile and requires bushwhacking to follow.

If you could trace it, you would have a 3-mile-long bushwhack adventure to the site of the Devorse Camp and the routes through it (section 79). This road is shown on the 1907 USGS surveys, but I have not explored it. I can only suggest that such a trip might make a good exercise for those wishing to test their skills with map and compass.

The footpath continues up along Groff Creek at least ½ mile above the fork, also becoming gradually less and less distinct. It can be followed all the way to a swampy, wooded area that appears on the USGS map and is the end of the path noted in the 1954 survey. A hunter I encountered on my trip here claimed that there was an old trail up Cathead, but if it is an extension of this route it is too indistinct to follow.

All of the stretch along Groff Creek is very beautiful walking. If you walk the full 3-mile distance to the swamp at the end of the footpath and allow plenty of time to explore along the waterfalls and the stream, you'll need more than four hours for the trek. The section of the road from the beginning of state land to the fork would be a very good ski-touring route.

This unique opening into the east portion of West Branch country offers several opportunities for bushwhacking to The Notch west and south or even due south to Cathead. But the ultimate trip in West Branch country would have to be a bush-whack from Groff Creek west to the site of the Devorse Camp, west and then south to Helldevil Dam, and finally west to Silver Lake and the Northville-Placid Trail. All of this route is suggested by the old roads and trails shown on the 1907 survey, but a back-packing bushwhack of this proportion is too difficult for all but a few hikers.

86 Toward King Vly
Bushwhack

North of Groff Creek a second steep valley cuts the mountains west of the Sacandaga. The valley points west toward King Vly, and a road through this draw was used to haul the timber logged there. The cliffs at the head of the draw were so steep that a road-way, protected overhead by hemlock boughs, was built to reduce ice and make the trip safe for horse-drawn sleighs. Stories of such a covered roadway induced me to explore the valley.

The cliffs are wonderfully steep, but without summer views. No signs of the covered roadway can be found. In summer, the valley is filled with mosquitoes and horse nettles and walking through it would be a disaster were it not the home of Braun's holly fern, an uncommon relative of the Christmas fern normally found only at a few sites in the Adirondack High Peaks. I know of no other south-ern Adirondack area where it is found. In winter, the valley is a large deer yarding area.

To reach the valley, begin on the Groff Creek Road (section 85). Before that road begins to climb around the north side of Groff Mountain, head north and cross Groff Creek. A gentle rise to the north separates Groff Creek valley from the desired draw. Head just north of west through the draw, which very soon becomes steep. It is sheltered by huge hemlock, and walking through the rise and the lower valley is easy for the forest is high and open, except for the patches of nettles.

As the valley narrows, the walking becomes very rough. A small intermittent stream flows through the draw and tumbles over a rocky course at its head. You will agree, once you reach it, that no wilder place can be found in a walk of less than two hours.

X
The Mayfield Hills

In the 1700s settlers pushed into the gently rolling hills north of the Mohawk to cultivate fields from Johnstown to Fish House on the Sacandaga. Northwest of the flood plain of the Sacandaga, the Mayfield Hills were their sentinel, guarding the lowlands, signaling the boundaries of their homesteads, and marking the borders of the distant impenetrable wilderness.

The Mayfield Hills continue to mark the southeastern boundary of the Adirondack wilds. Most of the land on the hills is now privately owned, but three destinations beckon hikers.

87 Feldspar Mine
Bushwhack along old road; hiking, snowshoeing

In the late 1800s and early 1900s, feldspar was mined in the Mayfield Hills and shipped to factories in New Jersey where it was ground to a very fine powder and used as a glaze for china. Also in the 1800s the Fonda, Johnstown, and Gloversville Railroad was extended to Northampton, a resort town now mostly flooded by Great Sacandaga Lake. A long conveyor belt was built from the feldspar mine on the Mayfield Hills to the railroad. Most of the old railroad route is now flooded by Great Sacandaga Lake, the conveyor belt has been removed, and even the cut for the mine is hidden from view.

The mine site, an amphitheater of pink rock, remains and can be reached by bushwhacking along abandoned roads. The land surrounding the route to the mine is owned by a paper company, and all access to this bushwhack has been recently posted, so hikers must obtain permission to walk this route.

To reach the mine, look for Mountain Road, which loops west

from Route 30, with one end 1 mile south of the Northville Bridge and the other 5¾ miles farther south. Cross Road, which is 1 mile long, connects Mountain Road and Route 30, intersecting the latter 5½ miles south of the Northville Bridge.

From the intersection of Mountain Road and Cross Road, drive north on Mountain Road for 1⅖ miles and park in the area of a sand pit. At the head of the sand pit is a recently posted but abandoned logging road, which intersects several other abandoned logging roads on the side of an unnamed hill in the Mayfield chain. One of these is the most direct route to the mine, but it cannot be used all the way as the lower, eastern, end is posted but not abandoned. With care, though, the road from the small sand pit can be used as a guide for the ⅘-mile, 660-foot, climb to the abandoned feldspar mine.

From the pit, the road heads northwest, following a creek. Then, in a small meadow, it turns southwest to round the mountain. There are several other logging roads, all less obvious, branching out at different points from the meadow. One heads north from the meadow and crosses the creek. Follow this one for 300 yards until it intersects another well-defined road. This was the original road to the mine and the land to the east, downhill, along it is posted. Use the road to continue northwest uphill.

Notice the deep ravine of the creek below on your left. Notice also the cement pillars that used to be stanchions for the cable that carried feldspar to the railroad. Just beyond, you will see the excavated area. Walls of pink orthoclase feldspar rim the basin. The beautiful pink circular wall drips with dark green mosses, kept moist by the stream flowing through the mine. The mine is at the head of the draw below the summit of the mountain. The exposed coarse-grained igneous rock also contains other feldspars, micas, and quartz, showing glacial striations.

The mine was worked into the 1920s and supplied ore to a 'modern' gravity-fed mill near Cranberry Creek in the vicinity of the present Route 30. When you return to the highway, look in the field east of the Old Red Barn Airport on Route 30. You will see the tailings from the old mine, huge conical piles of rock that accumulated beside the railroad right-of-way.

If you prefer views to geology, you could continue on the main logging road to the southwest. If you follow it south and then west and around the mountain, climbing its shoulder and then leaving the road to bushwhack toward the summit, you will find several overlooks with limited summer views. These are great in winter as destinations on a snowshoe trek.

88 Mud Pond and Overlook Cliff
Difficult bushwhack

The bushwhack route to Mud Pond and the cliff on a nearby unnamed knob begins on Warner Hill Road. To reach the start coming from the north, drive south on Route 30 for 1 mile from the Northville Bridge and turn right onto Mountain Road, which you then follow 2 miles to Warner Hill Road. Coming from the south, follow Mountain Road 2⅕ miles north from its intersection with Cross Road (section 87). Take Warner Hill Road northwest to the point where it crosses a creek, turns south, and becomes unsuited to all but four-wheel-drive vehicles. Park in the field north of the road before the bend and begin your bushwhack toward Mud Pond.

This bushwhack is difficult because there are no landmarks. You will have to follow a compass course toward magnetic north for over ¾ mile to reach Mud Pond. The bushwhack should take between forty-five minutes and one hour. The compass route takes you steeply up a little over 600 feet in ¾ mile, around the northeast side of a small knob, and then down 75 feet to the pond.

Mud Pond is a bog and is good for studying typical bog flora, when it is not flooded by beaver. There are remnants of a logging road around the far side, which you can use to walk around the pond.

On your return, climb to the knob and drop down to ledges that face the south side, almost ⅓ mile due south of the pond. From these ledges there is a fine view of Great Sacandaga Lake and Tamarack Swamp below. Now descend east of south to reach the valley and Warner Hill Road again. Note that this route requires experience and proficiency with the use of map and compass.

89 Cliffs behind Gifford Valley
Moderate bushwhack

The cliffs on an unnamed hill overlooking Gifford Valley offer better views of Great Sacandaga Lake than you will find on any other hilltop around the lake's long perimeter. Gifford Valley Road turns west of Route 30, just over 1 mile north of the Northville Bridge. Follow it for ⅘ mile, past a spit in Woodward Lake. Here there is a private driveway. Land west of the driveway belongs to

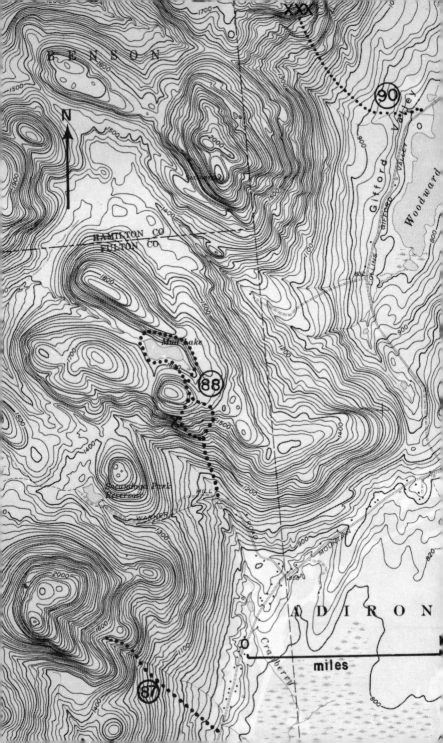

a paper company and is not posted. Your destination, the cliffs overlooking Gifford Valley, is on state land.

Southwest of the private driveway roadways lead into the interior from a gravel cleared area. These served the logging operations. Natives would tell you just to head up the mountain, but the route is not quite that simple. It is best to take a compass heading of 330 degrees magnetic. The cliffs, just under 1 mile away, are visible from the start of the road, facilitating a compass reading. Do not try to take the easiest route and follow the logging roads, for they generally do not lead in the desired direction. If you use one, make sure you compensate for variations in your compass course.

The heading should take you on a steep, 900-foot climb. The terrain is level just at the start and again just below the cliffs in a valley that is a natural wonder. Narrow-leafed spleenwort, maidenhair, grape fern, and many varieties of *Dryopteris* are mingled with several varieties of native orchids.

You should plan to climb to the valley's right, or northeast side, around the cliffs that rise vertically 70 feet from its floor. The climb is very rough and can be slippery when the mosses and leaves are wet. Use caution.

You should reach the top of the cliffs which ring the small mountain in an hour or so. Walk to the left, or southwest, to find the ledge with the best views. When you return, make sure you walk far enough around to the northeast before attempting to descend the steep area that extends well beyond the highest part of the cliffs.

The views are fantastic. A clear day is a must for this trip, for then you will be able to see a long sweep of Great Sacandaga Lake with its many islands. Sinclaire Point can be spotted beyond Northampton Beach Campsite and Maxon Ridge marks the distant horizon.

While the climb can be made in an hour, allow a half-day for the trek, planning for a picnic on the ridge and for time to explore the valley below the cliffs.

Do not forget to use a compass heading of 150 degrees from magnetic north on the return. You should intersect one of the logging roads, and with care you could pick up one to help with the return. Most lead generally toward Gifford Valley Road.

XI

The West Branch and Whitehouse

As early as 1835, settlers pushed west of the Sacandaga Valley to harvest the rich timber in the valley beside the West Branch of the Sacandaga, or the West River as it has always been known to natives. Several mills were constructed on the river to handle logs that were floated from as far away as Piseco and Arietta.

Today, the stretch of dirt and gravel road beside the West River is the only road into the wilderness of the West Branch spiral, and it offers a handsome introduction to the deep interior. Its destination, 8⅔ miles from Route 30, was the Whitehouse, a hunting and fishing camp. Log cabins surrounded a main house, but only the stone fireplaces remain. Drive the length of the road, stroll from its end along the West Branch, and become acquainted with the edge of the Adirondacks' deepest wilderness.

The trip to Whitehouse on the narrow road is an adventure in itself, even though it passes in part through land that has been recently timbered. Just south of the village of Wells on Route 30, Algonquin Drive heads west and crosses the outlet of Lake Algonquin within sight of the dam that created the lake from the Main Branch of the Sacandaga. West River Road forks left or south from Algonquin Drive, ¾ mile from Route 30, and continues southwest to Blackbridge, 2⅖ miles from Route 30.

From Blackbridge west, the road is narrow and driving speeds of twenty miles an hour are sufficient. Between Blackbridge and Jimmy Creek, the road is close to the river with great vistas across the rushing water and standing waves to the mountains that form this deep and scenic part of the gorge.

West of the bridge over Jimmy Creek a parking turnout on the south side of the road makes a good place to stop and enjoy the river. Beyond Jimmy Creek there is a steep hill where West River

Road can be especially bad, even for such a typical backcountry dirt road. From Jimmy Creek to Whitehouse the road is above and out of sight of the river.

Between Wells and Whitehouse the West Branch falls 300 feet as it tumbles through many sections of pretty rapids. Near Whitehouse and to the west, the river flows through a broader, flatter valley with two large, quiet eddies. Farther west are rapids and falls where the stream drops over 200 feet in a mile. This segment is described in sections 95 and 96.

Whitehouse is in a lovely, broad, upland valley with Dugway Mountain rising dramatically to the northeast. It provides an inviting center for all sorts of activities, especially hiking. The Northville-Placid Trail crosses the West Branch near Whitehouse on a magnificent new bridge. Fishermen and campers find adequate parking here, and hikers will find it the best jumping off place for the interior of the Silver Lake Wilderness.

Winter travelers should note that the road is plowed only to within 2 miles of Whitehouse. While skiers and snowshoers can enjoy the road, the additional 2 miles make it very difficult to reach the destinations described in this chapter, except as winter backpacking treks.

South of Wells, at the Sacandaga Public Campsite, the West Branch joins the main stream of the Sacandaga River, which continues to flow south, visible much of the way from Route 30. Along the river there are several picnic grounds and campsites, both private and public. With advance planning, hikers should be able to find accommodations in the area or locate a campsite suitable for enjoying the several walks in this chapter.

90 Jimmy Creek
Path; walking, fishing

Jimmy Creek tumbles over 400 feet in ¾ mile from the end of the long valley between Mount Dunham and Hamilton Mountain into the West Branch, which it meets 1½ miles west of Blackbridge. Its lovely series of small falls and cataracts and sparkling clear water are punctuated by a deep chute through folded rock ledges and a surprising waterfall that drops forty feet over a horizontally tiered headwall. The creek is secreted in a deep valley protected by towering hemlock.

Jimmy Creek

A narrow strip of private land that used to cut across the creek immediately north of the deepest part of the gorge has recently been acquired by the state, ensuring public access to the interior valley.

Photographers would enjoy the lower creek best before midday when sunlight can filter into the southeast-flowing water. Except for a short period in late morning, the creek lies in deep shade.

Park at the turnout west of the bridge over Jimmy Creek (see the introductory comments to this chapter). A very narrow strip of land north of the road and on both sides of the creek is privately owned. Hop rocks like fishermen do, for five minutes, or ask permission of the landholders to cross the 200 yards beside the creek. At this point you will see a well-defined footpath on the east side of the creek. Follow the path upstream or hop rocks on the shore for better views when the path swings back from the water.

It will take twenty minutes to walk to the beautiful sluice and another ten minutes to reach the deep pool below the falls. Note that the path is safely away from the tumbling water. It could be dangerous near them! The path climbs east around the falls to the ravine above and becomes increasingly faint as far as a sharp bend in the creek. You can reach the bend after forty-five minutes of walking from the road, but no one would walk that fast — there is far too much to enjoy!

Beyond the bend, the creek levels out and is less dramatic, but it still has good, deep woods on either side. You can either walk along the rocks in the creek or back in the high, open hemlock groves where witch hobble fills the forest floor. All signs of the path are gone, but even after it disappears, the walking is easy.

Boulders in the creek are tinged with the pink of feldspar and an occasional rock is studded with garnet. Near the falls, the sheer ledges are green and dripping with moss. On the return, notice the strange rock formation beside the pool below the falls. It is manmade, an old rock diversion wall to steer logs downstream below the falls. It is hard to imagine that this remote stream was ever used to float logs to mills below.

. Jimmy Creek is too splendid for all but the most leisurely visit. The climb beside it is so gentle that most people can enjoy the walk to the falls, one of the most brilliant gems in the southern Adirondacks.

91 Finch Mountain Cliffs
Bushwhack

There are so few cliffs with views within the area detailed by this guide that discovering a new one is a great thrill. Finch Mountain unquestionably has the best views of the West Branch Valley. Unfortunately the bushwhack to the cliffs is difficult, and access to the mountain depends on low water in the river. These deterrents can be overcome, and the result is an exciting adventure.

Park in the turnout west of the bridge over Jimmy Creek, 1½ miles west of Blackbridge (see introductory comments to this chapter). Access to the West Branch is down a short, 50-yard-long dirt road that leads to a log-based ford. The ford is too slippery for easy walking, even in very low water. Just upstream you can find a place where low water rock hopping is possible. Perhaps you should carry your hiking boots and wear an old pair of boots or even sneakers for the trip across the river. Note that in spring or in high water this sort of crossing is *impossible*. The West Branch is far too big a river and too much water flows over these rocks to make crossing safe except for a short time each summer. When the water is high, the current is too swift for a safe canoe or boat crossing. So, wait for a dry spell and then plan to take this trip.

Finch is a small cone-shaped mountain that rises 900 feet in a little over ½ mile from the river. After crossing the river, select a compass heading of 210 degrees magnetic. This route traverses the steep northwestern face of the mountain toward the summit. For the first 300 feet the climb is very steep and difficult, requiring the use of hands to scramble over the duff-covered tallus, which provides a very poor footing. Only a long trek from the east would avoid the scramble, so persevere. Above the first 300 feet, the climb is more gradual with huge glacial erratic blocks strewn across the gentler slopes. You will find that a few of the enormous erratics are quite remarkable.

Below the summit and to the west there is a series of small cliffs you can get around in order to reach the outcrops with the best views. However, it is easier simply to go over the summit and descend 40 feet to reach them. These are visible from West River Road 2¼ miles west of Jimmy Creek. You may encounter several small cliff tops before reaching the best one, from which there is a splendid view stretching from Dunham, Cutknife, Speculator, and Hamilton mountains on the north, past Dugway and Swart and the West Branch Valley to Three Sisters Mountain in the distant west.

Ninemile Creek Valley is clearly defined, cutting through the ridge that borders the West Branch Valley on the south.

Since the Hamilton Mountain fire tower is now closed, this perch is your only opportunity to view the hidden reaches of the Silver Lake Wilderness. The cliffs are sufficiently high to give you an eagle's perspective of the long West Branch Valley.

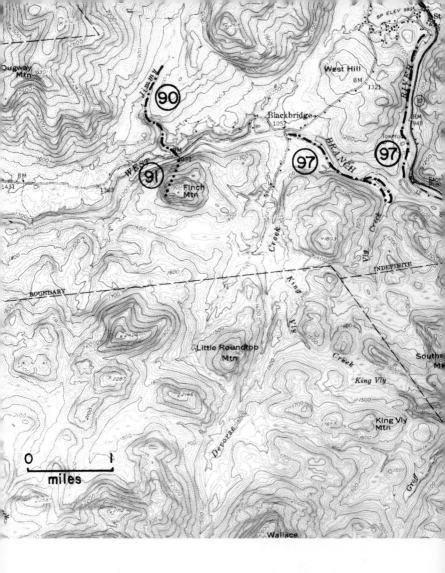

The round-trip bushwhack can be made in three hours. This does not offer ample time to enjoy the views. The return can be fairly easily directed, and it is best to retrace your steps. Watch the ledges along the last 300 feet on the return to the river. And again, do not attempt the trip at all if water in the West Branch is not sufficiently low to provide a safe crossing.

203

92 Rapids on the West Branch
Abandoned road; walking, picnicking

Halfway between Blackbridge and Whitehouse two short paths head from West River Road toward the West Branch, each following abandoned logging roads. The first is on private land and is posted, but the second is on Forest Preserve lands and is delightful. It leaves West River Road (see introductory comments to this chapter) 4⅓ miles west of Blackbridge and heads south toward the river. You will notice the road turning left as you cross a small knoll. Park opposite the road on the north side of West River Road; there is also room for one car on the side of the abandoned road, a short distance from the turnout.

The road descends gently to a shelf above the river, and then continues steeply down to the river itself in a very beautiful and wild section. The little island shown on the 1954 USGS map here no longer exists, so perhaps it was only a large gravel bar that has since washed away.

A steel cable stretches across the river between trees on either side. It is the remains of a gauging station that used to measure the flow of the river. Such cables are also used by hunters to carry gear to the river's far side.

This is a short pleasant path, with a grade easy enough for the occasional walker. Because it is along an old road, it is wide and dry enough to use after a rain when the woods might be too wet. It also brings you to an ideal picnic spot, where there are several rocks for sitting along the shore.

93 Ninemile Creek
Path; walking, camping

In low water, the path to Ninemile Creek falls offers a short and easy fifteen-minute walk. In high water, the trip is impossible, so pick a midsummer dry spell for this outing. Only then will hopping rocks to cross the West Branch of the Sacandaga be a safe and dry adventure.

Ninemile Creek joins the West Branch 200 yards east of the cable described in section 92. Crossing in the vicinity of the cable is easiest. Near the end of the cable on the south shore, the path angles south to intersect the creek and then follows it ½ mile to the falls. It also neatly avoids the low land brush near the confluence.

South, upstream from the falls, it is easy to hop rocks and continue along the creek for quite a distance. The entire 1½-mile stretch in which the creek drops nearly 400 feet from the escarpment south of the West Branch is a delightful wilderness trip. It is just unfortunate that the falls and creek are at their best when the West Branch is too high to ford safely.

94 Canary Pond
Trail; hiking, camping

From Whitehouse, the Northville-Placid Trail approaches Canary Pond to the south through marvelously rugged woods, said to be the best timbered forests along the entire length of the trail. The hike is certainly a must on anyone's list of walks into West Branch country, but in spite of the well-groomed trail, it is so long it is almost too difficult for a one-day trip.

There is no longer a lean-to at Mud Lake to break the trek to Canary Pond so for those who do not backpack, the 13⅕-mile round-trip walk would be a strenuous one-day outing. If you choose to camp along the way, then you certainly should begin at the south end of the trail (section 77), walk to Silver Lake, camp at the lean-to there, and continue the next day on the 2¹/₁₀-mile section to Canary Pond and then north following the rest of the route described here. The level 2-mile stretch of wilderness between Silver Lake and Canary Pond is enjoyable, but can hardly be included in a one-day walk.

The round-trip to Canary Pond from the north has the advantage of following one of the few trails in the deep northwest part of West Branch country. The trail heads south through the remote valley to the east of Moose Mountain. This relatively level route does not always give a true impression of how tremendously rugged the surrounding mountains are.

The trail is, of course, well marked. Just west of the Whitehouse parking area, the marked left fork directs you south to the new bridge over the river. For 1½ miles the route is a gentle rise to the south. It then bears southwest to the only really steep grade. This is a climb of 200 feet in a ½ mile up a draw, followed by a gentle descent of 200 feet over 1 mile to Mud Lake. The lean-to at Mud Lake was recently destroyed by fire, and although it is scheduled to be replaced, it is still out as of this writing.

The trail circles the west end of Mud Lake and then heads southeast to round Moose Mountain. It follows a small brook gently upstream for a time and then crosses it. Canary Pond is 6⅗ miles from Whitehouse and has a good spot for a picnic, even if the shores are a bit swampy. It is a fisherman's delight and a worthy destination for the walk through the most majestic forests of West Branch country.

95 Falls on the West Branch
Path; hiking, camping

Of all the walks into the wilderness bordered by the West Branch, this one is certainly the most dramatic. In fact, the scenery is so extraordinary it may have no equal in the whole Adirondacks.

Much can be said of the West Branch and its many moods, most of which are expressed in this one walk. The river is quiet by Big Eddy, fierce through the rapids and the gorge beside the falls, and then hidden and mysterious beneath towering cliffs.

No matter what the weather or the time of year, it is a long and difficult walk. In early spring when the river is wildest, the trip to the falls is almost impossible. In midsummer, when the water is low, the stream is less exciting, but the walking is easier. The rugged tumbles of boulders are certainly enhanced by large flows of water, but the impressive scenery is not totally dependent on them.

The trip to the falls begins west of Whitehouse and follows the Northville-Placid Trail northwest for ⅘ mile to a fork. The way right, which heads north, is the Northville-Placid Trail and is well marked. The left fork is a path that follows an abandoned logging road west for ⅗ mile to Hamilton Lake Stream. The route is very wide, flat, and easy to walk.

Hamilton Lake Stream is a principal cause of the difficulties on this walk. The cable bridge over the stream has proved difficult to maintain, and in high water, the crossing can be wet. In low water, though, you can hop dryly across on exposed rocks.

Beyond the crossing, the path heads southwest toward the river. The first glimpse of the eddies on the river is so lovely you will wish the path had been closer to the river all the way west from Whitehouse. Beyond, upstream, it stays by the water's edge for nearly 1 mile, past the first eddy, a series of rapids, Big Eddy, and on to the outlet of Cold Brook. In the last ½ mile, the route is a

Falls on the West Branch of the Sacandaga

fisherman's path, for the old road did not extend this far west.

From Cold Brook west, the valley narrows so that in places steep cliffs rise directly from the river bed. The path at first clings to the steep shore, then almost disappears, so that it seems easier to hop along rocks at the water's edge. After the first big bend with its deep pool and cliffs on the south, it is definitely easier, in low water, to walk along the edge of the river.

In the ½ mile west of Cold Brook there is no quiet water; a crescendo of rapids leads to the first falls. Behind the falls, cliffs on the north shore rise 200 feet above the river. On their crests are huge white pines, which make the cliffs seem even taller. If you look back east along the rapids, you will see many of these huge pines dotting the shoreline.

You can climb, with some difficulty, around the great boulders on the north side of the falls to reach the second falls, only 200 yards upstream. The trek between the falls is so difficult that it can take as much as forty-five minutes. Although the beauty of the second falls justifies the trip, it is recommended for only the most agile and prudent. In high water, it is necessary to climb the cliffs to continue along the river.

The second falls are even narrower and higher than the first, and both are pretty, even in low water. The enormous boulders that line the gorge attest to nature's past violence, but there are signs of recent furies. Perhaps you can spot the shattered hulk of an old rowboat fifteen feet high on a rock ledge. It underscores the temper of the river and illustrates the vast amount of water it carries and the huge area it drains.

There are few difficulties encountered on the return trip that are not met on the outward walk, with the exception of tired feet and legs. With time to rest and picnic and photograph, you can easily spend six hours on this hike.

96 West Branch Gorge
Difficult bushwhack; camping

The pair of waterfalls on the West Branch 3 miles west of Whitehouse stand at the eastern edge of the deepest part of the river's gorge, with formidable cliffs deterring travel farther west. Tales of another waterfall tempted me to explore the hidden recesses of the wild river. In the years since the first edition of this guide appeared, I have walked many places in the Adirondacks and explored routes for three more guides, but no trip was as wonderful as the walk through the West Branch Gorge, when I discovered not one but three more waterfalls. A bushwhack along the river is as challenging and exciting as any you might attempt. I recommend this route as a one-day through-trek, starting at Whitehouse early in the morning. You will complete the bushwhack just before nightfall, coming out on Route 10 via the path along Piseco Outlet (section 71).

In high water much of the trip has to be walked on the edge of the gorge, too far back or high up to appreciate the river. Only in very low water is it possible to hop rocks and follow the river's course between eddies and falls.

Since the river falls 300 vertical feet in a distance of 2 miles, it might seem prudent to walk downstream, downhill through the gorge. I find it preferable to walk from east to west, upstream, so as to approach the river's several falls from below. There are truly beautiful places to camp on the trip through, and the length of the trip makes camping desirable. If you plan to camp, the best approach is from the east, walking as far as the second pair of falls, where there is a good campsite.

Beyond the first pair of falls (section 95), the river tumbles through a dark-walled ravine where even at noon the deep green of overhanging hemlock and pines brings dusk to the river. A series of deep pools accompany you ¼ mile west, and then the river makes a big bend to the southwest. Here the channel is so narrow and strong that it may be necessary to climb out of the gorge, even in low water.

The third waterfall appears as the river banks become less steep. When you first spot the third falls, look sharply, for the fourth falls is hiding scarcely 200 yards upstream from it. There is a deep pool below each. The walls beside the upper pool make traveling so difficult that you'll need almost forty-five minutes to walk between the two falls; even more time and agility than is required for the trip between the first pair of falls.

On the bank on the north shore above the fourth falls a marvelous campsite is obviously well used. It is high on a hemlock-protected ledge covered with a deep cushion of moss and creeping white winterberry. A rudimentary path leads west from the campsite along the river.

Above the fourth falls, there is another beautiful eddy, and above it, a fifth cataract, just west of the outlet of Owl Pond. Hunters' paths can be found on the north shore west of the eddy. Beyond the westernmost rapids, the river is broad, and there are no more paths on the north shore. Walking along it is very difficult for it is rimmed with dense alder swamps. Paths make walking on the south shore a bit easier — they emanate from a hunting camp secreted in the wilderness on the south shore. However, they end before you reach the confluence of the West Branch and Piseco Outlet. Without a canoe, the only way out is to swim the river in the quiet water near the confluence. If you can cross the river and reach the west shore of Piseco Outlet, it is a simple matter to pick up the extension of the North Vly path (section 71). Use it to reach Route 10.

If the thought of swimming the West Branch does not appeal to you, make your way along the north shore to Piseco Outlet and upstream along the outlet to the area of the islands, where it is possible to ford that stream. Rough going should be anticipated in the alders beside the river; unfortunately walking back from its border is little better.

Allow three hours for the walk from Whitehouse to the first pair of waterfalls, an hour and a half for the walk to the second pair, an hour to reach Owl Pond outlet, less than an hour for the trek to the last cataract, an hour for the walk along the south shore of the flow to the Piseco Outlet confluence, and an hour and a half to swim the river and walk out to Route 10. This total of nine hours is easily extended to ten or more to allow time for lunch and photographs. Walking is so difficult in places that distances do not convey a true sense of the difficulty involved. You will travel at least 7 miles on the bushwhack. This remote adventure through a valley whose grandeur is unrivaled in the southern Adirondacks is extraordinarily difficult, a fact which will leave the gorge untouched and unspoiled for years to come.

97 Along the West and Main Branches of the Sacandaga

Dirt roads; walking, cross-country skiing

Walking along little traveled dirt roads can be the best way to watch for birds and enjoy the scenery. Two sections of roads south of Wells are ideal.

Drive southwest from Wells to Blackbridge and cross the river. The road straight ahead, south, is heavily posted, but a left turn, to the east, takes you on a dirt road that ends on a loop in the Wilderness Area. The road is adjacent to the West Branch but out of sight of it and leads to a point opposite the Sacandaga Campsite.

In summer it offers birds, berries, and butterflies; in winter it offers a chance for easy cross-country skiing.

The road reaches the Wilderness Area within 1 mile of Black-bridge, and then makes a loop just over 1 mile long. A short side path to Vly Creek leaves the road 400 yards before the eastern-most part of the loop.

Even prettier is the 1½-mile walk along the dirt surface section of the road on the west side of the Main Branch of the Sacandaga south of Wells. Cross the outlet of Lake Algonquin and take the first left turn to the south. Park beyond the surfaced road. No matter what the weather, walking close to the Sacandaga is thrilling: colorful in autumn, quiet in summer, wild in the late winter or early spring, when snowshoes or cross-country skis may be necessary.

XII
Gilmantown Road

At the end of the eighteenth century, settlers began to move to the community of Wells on the Main Branch of the Sacandaga and build saw mills to harvest the rich timber in the surrounding mountains. Today the hills around Lake Algonquin bear the names of some of the early settlers, the Overackers, who were among the first; Pettit, for years a hotel-keeper in the community; and the Dunhams.

A road existed from Wells north to Lake Pleasant as early as 1805, but the War of 1812 saw the designing of the "Old Military Road" from Albany to Sacketts Harbor, on the shores of Lake Ontario. The road went through the communities of Northville and Hope to Wells. At Wells, it headed northwest beside Elbow Creek, and past Charley and Mud lakes to the outlet of Lake Pleasant. Beyond Lake Pleasant, the road headed through Wilcox Clearing to follow the Miami and Cedar rivers, and approached Raquette Lake. The course was said to be along an old Indian trail and the road was supposed to have been laid out with "considerable engineering skill." The section from Wells to Lake Pleasant was an important highway link and was the principal route north until a road was constructed near the present Route 30; but the portion of the road north of Lake Pleasant had grown to brush and was impassable except on foot as early as 1820.

In 1835, David Dunning acquired the land around the pond east of Gilmantown Road that bears his name. He built a saw mill there and operated it through the 1860s.

The Gilmantown Road remained the main road between Wells and Lake Pleasant until the end of the nineteenth century, although work on the road that is now "Old Route 30" was started in 1862.

When gold rush fever hit the Adirondacks in the 1880s, prospectors claimed to have found gold on Elbow Creek and a mine shaft was dug. Gold and silver were never mined successfully, but countless companies sold shares and were organized to seek out the precious metals everyone thought had to be in the mountains.

Today, the Gilmantown Road invites hikers to several adventures. Each adventure would be enhanced by reading the chapter on Wells in Aber and King's *The History of Hamilton County*, from which these background notes on the Gilmantown Road were taken. To find the road, drive north on Route 30, ¼ mile past the bridge over the Sacandaga at the north end of Lake Algonquin and the community of Wells. Gilmantown Road is a left turn from Route 30. The road leads up the hill between Mount Overrocker and Pettit Mountain. Part of the land beside Elbow Creek is posted, but there are several clearly marked sections of Forest Preserve land where you might wish to stop for a picnic.

98 Pettit Mountain Cliffs
Easy bushwhack; hiking, picnicking

Drive north of Route 30 on Gilmantown Road for 1½ miles. Here the road crosses Elbow Creek. The east shore is posted, but 200 yards south, opposite two distinctive boulders edging the west side of the road, Elbow Creek is clearly marked as state land. From this point, it is possible to make a very steep but rewarding climb to the cliffs on Pettit Mountain.

The route is generally east up the face of the mountain. The first 200 feet or so to the power line are precipitous but not dangerous. Continue east past the power line, climbing until the lower cliffs are visible. The easiest route is to the right, south, around the cliffs.

You will reach a shelf from which there are several vantage points. Continue northeast across the shelf to the second range of cliffs. Walk north, left, beyond the cliffs before attempting to scale them to the summit. The entire summit area is steep, but the cliffs on the south face are too vertical to scale. At that, you will find you have to scramble to attain the summit from the northwest.

Cross the spruce-covered summit to the exposed ledges on the south. Overactive campers have done some damage to the summit and cleared walkways through the spruce cover.

The views are fantastic: north, up Elbow Creek Valley toward

View from Pettit Mountain

Speculator Mountain, west to Hamilton, Cutknife, and Round mountains, across Lake Algonquin and the Sacandaga Valley to Cathead, Wallace, and Three Ponds mountains in the south-southwest, and east to the range of small hills with cliffs beyond the Sacandaga to Hadley and Roundtop on the distant horizon.

The cliffs are high! Stay back from the edge. Return with care, retracing the route to avoid dangerous ledges. The climb, 400 feet in a little more than ¼ mile, will seem incredibly steep, but commensurate with the rewards for the forty-five minutes of climbing. The return can be made in twenty minutes.

99 Elbow Creek
Old road; walking

Elbow Creek drains the valley between Cutknife and Hamilton mountains. The valley served as the route of an old logging road along which a visible footpath can still be found. Starting just north of the Wells Reservoir, the road heads west through private

214

lands for ½ mile, although state land touches the road in several spots. The roadside is littered with several old jeeps.

When you come to the end of the obvious road you will see a cottage ahead and to the right. Turn left just before the house and take the first right. Old logging roads always trace a confusing maze, and this is no exception. If you do not find that right turn, you will start going uphill.

Notice that the road has a rock base in some places. A little clearing of blowdowns and deadfalls would turn this into an excellent cross-country ski trail.

After a fifteen-minute walk beyond the private land, the road disappears in a wet area. Stay left, north and high, and you will come to the roadway again within 100 feet. After another five minutes of walking, you will approach a stream that drains an obvious draw on the northeast flank of Hamilton Mountain. Notice hunters' blazes on the trees; these slashes indicate the stream crossing. The continuing road and path is 100 feet upstream on the west bank. The route is now close to Elbow Creek, which lies in the valley below to the right. After another five-minute walk, you cross an intermittent stream. Beyond, there are several beaver flows in the valley. If you walk away from the path you will see old beaver works and a huge beaver house.

After walking twenty minutes more you will cross Elbow Creek and continue on the north side. The roadway is still obvious and continues north of beaver meadows and swampy areas to connect with the Hamilton Mountain Trail.

Hikers who are used to following old roads could reach the Hamilton Mountain Trail from Gilmantown Road in two and a half hours. The distance is under 3½ miles. The Elbow Creek path intersects the Hamilton Mountain Trail south of the part of the latter trail that is now closed to the public.

The fire tower on Hamilton Mountain has been removed, so the views are gone. Since the summit is densely covered in spruce, there is only one small view to the north from a narrow opening below the summit. The views of the Silver Lake Wilderness from the tower on this mountain have always been favorites with hikers; the closing is unfortunate. Even though it is possible to find the new, longer route to the mountain and avoid the private posted lands around Hamilton Lake, there is little reason now to make the 1,200-foot, 1½-mile climb.

So, although you could use the Elbow Creek route to reach Hamilton Mountain, the road seems best for just a walk in the woods or a cross-country ski trek.

100 Dunning Pond
Trail; hiking

A 4⅓-mile-long snowmobile trail runs from Gilmantown Road past Dunning Pond, along the pond's outlet, and then through the woods on a newly cut route to an old logging road that intersects Route 30 just north of Dunning Creek. Both the eastern and western parts of the trail follow old logging roads.

The eastern terminus of the trail is on Route 30, just ⅓ mile south of the Route 8 bridge over the Sacandaga. To find the western, unmarked, trailhead, drive ¾ mile north of Charley Lake to Dunning Creek bridge. Then retrace your route for ⅕ mile and look for a post and the beginning of the trail concealed on the east side of the road.

The trail follows a course generally east from Gilmantown Road for 9/10 mile toward Dunning Pond, contouring around the hill south of the pond. You can see water glinting in the distance through the trees. As the trail swings south near the outlet, you will come to the easiest access to the pond. There are signs of an old road, a stone bridge, and foundations on a spruce-covered

rise between the trail and the outlet. This is the site of the mill operated by David Dunning in the middle of the nineteenth century. Now the pond is a nearly dry meadow filling with swampy shrubs.

The next 1½ miles are most lovely, for the route is close to the south shore of the creek. The beautiful woods and high mixed forest with some outstanding hemlock shelter a rich understory of ferns and mosses. The outlet has a few little rapids interspersed with deep pools, and there is one small waterfall.

The trail along the south side of the stream is poorly marked but easy to follow, with a few wet places to traverse. You will reach a washed out snowmobile bridge at the end of a still water, and within ¼ mile of the bridge the creek begins to fall steeply toward Route 30.

You can follow the trail to the old logging road, which descends to Route 30, although the newly cut part is difficult to find because of inadequate marking. It heads due north from the creek, climbing the hillside to intersect the old road. The road winds downhill toward Route 30 through good mixed hardwood forest, and walking this section is pleasant. The creek is below, south, of the logging road, deep in the hemlock-covered ravine and out of sight of the road. You can hear it in one or two places near Route 30, but most of the time the trail is disappointingly too far away. The section from the snowmobile bridge to Route 30 is slightly circuitous and covers 2 miles in a descent of almost 700 feet to the highway.

The trip described so far assumes that you have arranged to have cars at both ends. There is an even better way to enjoy the creek. With one car, walk in from Gilmantown Road to the bridge and back one day, and make a second trip up from Route 30 to the washed-out bridge a second day. Then, instead of retracing your steps on the logging road, follow the creek to Route 30. Of course, this is easiest accomplished in low water.

East of the snowmobile bridge, the creek begins a precipitous drop with the most beautiful rock slides and small pools. The upper part is a dramatic series of small falls and lovely boulders. Sometimes you can hop rocks in the stream bed; sometimes you will have to improvise a route beside the creek. Pick the early part of a bright blue day for a walk down the creek and be rewarded by a tapestry of multicolored reflecting pools below large shelves of boulder-strewn walls. The steep banks of the ravine that shelters the lower part of the creek keeps it quiet and secluded, even as it approaches Route 30.

You will find the Berry bublet fern, *Cystopteris bulbiferous,* growing on the ledges near the highway. Their presence indicates limestone in the rocks.

If you walk through from Gilmantown Road to Route 30 following the trail all the way, you will need less than three hours. If you follow the trail to the bridge and then bushwhack along the creek, you can easily spend four hours on the trek. If you climb from Route 30 to the stream you will need an hour and a quarter for the walk to the washed-out snowmobile bridge. You can walk from here west to Dunning Pond and back in two hours more. The trip down the creek back to Route 30 will take at least two hours. No matter what way you approach the creek, you will have a beautiful full day's adventure.

XIII
Driving Trips

It may seem inappropriate to mention a motorized trip in a trail guide; however, one of my greatest pleasures has been to escort older friends who can no longer enjoy a forest walk on drives into almost wilderness areas. There are several routes so remote that they substitute for very active hikes. All are on public roads. Any one of these would also make a good introduction for newcomers and set the stage for further explorations.

The most obvious route is along the Powley-Piseco Road (see Chapter I for details on mileages). You may want to detour to the East Canada Creek along the road described in sections 1 and 2. Farther north stop along the bridge over North Creek and enjoy the views from it and notice the roadside plants just to its north. The entire stretch of dirt road beside the East Canada is lovely, even from a car, especially the part near the confluence of Brayhouse Brook (section 5), where you will find the best picnic place on the road. The bridge at Powley Place also has a beautiful vista, both up and down the North Branch. I have even watched deer in the stream while I was standing on the bridge. Farther north the road is edged with sheer cliffs between East and West Notch Mountains. Look carefully in the trees beside the road — you can expect to see owls.

Route 10 just north of Pine Lake has its treasures, one being the beaver houses established near the road in a swamp not ¼ mile from the intersection with Route 29. The swamps north of here come almost to the road and with little effort ferns and other unusual plants are easy to see. At the first bend in the road, you can look into Stoner Lake Outlet and find, in August, a stand of Cardinal flowers. The walk to the gorge (section 51) is not too much to add to a driving trip.

The drive along Route 10 in Hamilton County is unrivaled in the Adirondacks. There are many places along it from which to see the West Branch of the Sacandaga. Many of the valley's pleasures are visible from the road and are described in Chapter VII, which also gives mileages along the road. I happen to think that dawn is the best time to see the river. The combinations of mist and reflections and slanting light are spectacular. Fall colors are always best here.

In late summer you will enjoy the sight of dew-covered cobwebs glistening in the morning sun from high branches of trees silhouetted against the softness of the fog-shrouded swamps. I have three favorite places to stop and enjoy the river and photograph. One is at the "second bridge" north of Arietta; both sides of the bridge over the river are perfectly framed with trees and hills so the reflections in the quiet river double the scene in perfect symmetry. Another is south of Trout Lake Mountain where the meadow is always filled with a riot of color. Stop where State Brook flows under the road. The third is south of Shaker Place where the road has been widened; here are the best places to view the flows along the West Branch.

You should enjoy an autumn drive around the loop formed by the trip west from Pine Lake along Route 29A, north of the Powley-Piseco Road to Route 10, and back south along the West Branch to Pine Lake. Because of the preponderance of swamp maples, the fall colors here are unsurpassed in the Adirondacks.

East of Caroga Lake there are several dirt roads heading south from Benson Road. One, which is 2¾ miles from the intersection of the Benson Road and Route 10, leads to the site of the oldest Catholic Church in Fulton County. In the cemetery near the site, there are not only many old headstones to delight historians but there are also some of the largest blueberries to be found anywhere.

Route 30 commands many views across the lower Sacandaga. This stretch combined with a drive up the road to Whitehouse becomes a beautiful excursion. See Chapter XI for details. You could picnic along the West Branch near Jimmy Creek or at Whitehouse. Remember that the dirt road often erodes badly in late winter, so driving it in early spring before it has been regraded can be difficult. Roads south along the Sacandaga also make good driving excursions (see section 97).

You will also want to drive north from Wells along Gilmantown Road. Chapter XII gives the brief history of that section. Stop along Elbow Creek for a picnic.

Dew on spider web

Every fall, you ought to enjoy a trip around the "Big Horn" as natives of the fringes of the Adirondacks call the trip up Route 30 from the Mohawk Valley, west on Route 8, and south on Route 10. You might question why the circular route is called a trip around the horn, but there is a logical local explanation. At the very southern edge of the Adirondacks in the town of Caroga, the Cape Horn Road follows the Caroga Creek after making a sharp angle with Route 29. That angle, which resembled the horn of South America, inspired the naming of the road. In the early twentieth century, a drive from Johnstown north to the edges of the Mountains circling around the Cape Horn Road became a trip around the "Little Horn." With the advent of automobiles and longer Sunday excursions, the drive north to Speculator and Piseco became the trip around the "Big Horn."

References
and Other
Resources

References

Aber, Ted and Stella King. *The History of Hamilton County.* Lake Pleasant, NY: Great Wilderness Books, 1965.

McMartin, Barbara. *Caroga: The Town Recalls Its Past.* Caroga, NY: Town of Caroga, 1976.

Rickett, Harold William. *Wild Flowers of the United States: The Northeastern States,* vol. 1. New York: The New York Botanical Garden and McGraw-Hill Book Company, 1966.

Simms, Jeptha R. *Trappers of New York, or a Biography of Nicholas Stoner and Nathaniel Foster.* Albany, NY: J. Munsell, 1857.

Wherry, Edgar T. *The Fern Guide: Northeastern and Midland United States and Adjacent Canada.* Philadelphia: The Morris Aboretum of the University of Pennsylvania, 1972.

Other Sources

For information on plants in the Adirondacks, send for the mimeographed "List of Rare and Endangered Plants," available from the New York State Department of Environmental Conservation, 50 Wolf Road, Albany, NY 12233.

For trail information, contact the following:

Department of Environmental Conservation, Northville, New York 12134.

Office of Tourism, Town of Lake Pleasant, Speculator, New York, 12164.

Adirondack Mountain Club, 172 Ridge Street, Glens Falls, New York 12801.

Chamber of Commerce, Fulton County, Main Street, Gloversville, New York 12078.

222

For other recreational information, as noted, contact the following:
    For "I Love New York" brochures, camping guides, the "State Travel Guide," and maps, contact the New York State Department of Commerce, Albany, New York 12245.
    For the brochures and guides: "The Adirondack Adventure," "Adirondack Area Fishing Waters," "Adirondack Area Map and Information Guide," "North Country Craft Trails Map," "Off-the-Beaten-Path," (Scenic Roads), and "The Historic Adirondacks," contact the Adirondack Association, Adirondack, New York 12808.

Guidebooks from New Hampshire Publishing Company

Written for people of all ages and experience, these highly popular and carefully prepared books feature detailed trail directions, notes on points of interest, sketch maps, and photographs.

For New York State —

Discover the Adirondacks, 1: From Indian Lake to the Hudson River, by Barbara McMartin. $6.95
Fifty Hikes in the Adirondacks, by Barbara McMartin. $7.95
25 Walks in the Finger Lakes Region, by Bill Ehling. $5.95
25 Ski Tours in the Adirondacks, By Almy and Anne Coggeshall. $5.95

In the Fifty Hikes series —

Fifty Hikes in Central Pennsylvania, by Tom Thwaites. $6.95
Fifty Hikes in Vermont, by Ruth and Paul Sadlier. $7.95
Fifty Hikes in the White Mountains, by Daniel Doan. $6.95
Fifty Hikes in Maine, by John Gibson. $6.95
Fifty More Hikes in Maine, by Cloe Catlett. $6.95
Fifty Hikes in Connecticut, by Gerry and Sue Hardy. $6.95

Other guides —

20 Bicycle Tours in Vermont, by John S. Freidin. $5.95
Canoeing Massachusetts, Rhode Island and Connecticut, by Ken Weber. $6.95
25 Ski Tours in the Green Mountains, by Sally and Daniel Ford. $4.95

Available from bookstores, sporting goods stores, or the publisher. For complete descriptions of these and other skiing, hiking, walking, canoeing, and bicycling guides for the Northeast, write to New Hampshire Publishing Company, Box 70, Somersworth, NH 03878.